Swedes in Michigan

DISCOVERING THE PEOPLES OF MICHIGAN

Arthur W. Helweg, Russell M. Magnaghi, and Linwood H. Cousins, *Series Editors*

Ethnicity in Michigan: Issues and People
Jack Glazier and Arthur W. Helweg

Discovering the Peoples of Michigan is a series of publications examining the state's rich multicultural heritage. The series makes available an interesting, affordable, and varied collection of books that enables students and educated lay readers to explore Michigan's ethnic dynamics. A knowledge of the state's rapidly changing multicultural history has far-reaching implications for human relations, education, public policy, and planning. We believe that Discovering the Peoples of Michigan will enhance understanding of the unique contributions that diverse and often unrecognized communities have made to Michigan's history and culture.

Swedes in Michigan

Rebecca J. Mead

Michigan State University Press

East Lansing

♾ The paper used in this publication meets the minimum requirements
of ANSI/NISO Z39.48-1992 (R 1997) (Permanence of Paper).

Michigan State University Press
East Lansing, Michigan 48823-5245

Printed and bound in the United States of America.

18   17   16   15   14   13   12   1   2   3   4   5   6   7   8   9   10

LIBRARY OF CONGRESS CATALOGING-IN-PUBLICATION DATA
Mead, Rebecca J.
Swedes in Michigan / Rebecca J. Mead.
p. cm. — (Discovering the peoples of Michigan)
Includes bibliographical references and index.
ISBN 978-1-61186-041-2 (pbk. : alk. paper) 1. Swedes—Michigan—History.
2. Swedish Americans—Michigan—History. 3. Immigrants—Michigan—History.
I. Title.
F575.S23M43 2012
977.40043'97—dc23
2011031295

Cover design by Ariana Grabec-Dingman
Book design by Charlie Sharp, Sharp Des!gns, Lansing, Michigan

Cover photo: Swedish Christmas Celebration, Detroit, Michigan, 1939.
Courtesy Walter P. Reuther Library, Wayne State University.

Michigan State University Press is a member of the Green Press Initiative and
is committed to developing and encouraging ecologically responsible publishing practices. For more information about the Green Press Initiative and the use
of recycled paper in book publishing, please visit *www.greenpressinitiative.org*.

Visit Michigan State University Press at *www.msupress.org*

Contents

Introduction

The first Swedish immigrants to the United States arrived in 1638, settling in and around the area of what is now Wilmington, Delaware, and parts of Pennsylvania. At that time, Sweden was a formidable imperial force apparently with the resources to support colonial settlement and trade. The early colonies struggled, however, because they were expensive and few settlers could be induced to emigrate. The Swedish colonies were captured by the Dutch in 1655, transferred to England when the English took over the Dutch North American colonies in 1660, and finally became part of William Penn's new colony of Pennsylvania in 1682. Subsequently, emigration from Sweden was discouraged by punitive legislation in order to conserve labor and other resources for domestic purposes.[1]

By the mid-1800s, Sweden was a politically and economically progressive country, but its power in the Baltic region and in Europe had declined as a result of war and the growing influence of Russia. In addition, internal political and religious tensions, large population increase, famine, and agricultural dislocation motivated 1.2 million Swedes to migrate to the United States between 1851 and 1930, one-fourth of them between 1868 and 1893. Prior to the Civil War, approximately one-third of the fifteen thousand immigrants were families, mostly farmers and craftsmen who had the financial resources necessary for the enterprise. After the war ended, the numbers increased dramatically: 103,000 arrived between 1868 and 1873; 475,000 between 1880 and 1893; and more than 200,000 between 1893 and 1897, despite the serious depression in the United States during these years. The emigration of so many people had profound consequences both for Sweden and for the countries that became home to Swedish immigrants.[2]

Changing circumstances in both countries meant that different groups of people relocated for a variety of reasons over time. In early years, many Swedes were dissatisfied with the established Lutheran Church, which required that everyone to be a member and pay tithes. Until 1858 it was illegal to belong to any other church, and Swedish dissenters faced discrimination and government persecution. The early nineteenth century was a period of religious revivalism in many countries, and the Church of Sweden faced many challenges from alternative religious groups. It is estimated that perhaps 10 percent of the earliest emigrants left Sweden seeking religious freedom. In some areas of the Midwest, new communities were established when entire congregations immigrated with their pastors. While this trend was not so evident in Michigan, Swedish immigrants to the state often moved as individuals for the same reason. Beginning in the 1860s Swedish laws were changed to limit the political power of the established church, but the introduction of high property qualifications for voting disfranchised many lower-class Swedes. In the United States, in contrast, male immigrants could vote once they became naturalized citizens—and even in some states when they filed their "first papers" or official declarations of their intention to become citizens. In addition, some young men wished to avoid obligatory military service.[3]

By far the most significant reason Swedes emigrated to the United States, however, was Sweden's deteriorating economic situation, especially in agriculture. Between 1750 and 1850, the population of Sweden doubled and land became scarce, so even relatively prosperous farms could not support large families. Throughout most of the nineteenth century, the vast majority of Swedish emigrants were farmers and agricultural laborers who could not find work and who had no hope of acquiring land in Sweden. From the 1830s to the late 1860s, land speculation, enclosure, and a series of crop failures led to bankruptcies and famine, displacing almost half of Sweden's farmers by 1870. In the 1880s the situation worsened as the opening of new farm lands in the United States (and other countries) and mechanization drastically reduced prices and caused an agricultural depression. In this decade alone, approximately seven percent of the Swedish population emigrated to the United States. In contrast to the families who constituted most of the pre-Civil War migration, most of the Swedes who came to the United States after 1880 were young, single people (male and female in roughly equal numbers, often in groups of friends or relatives).

Young men and women who had no future in Sweden had to seek opportunities elsewhere, and they were attracted to the United States by higher wages and the availability of land. The case of one Michigan immigrant was typical. He arrived with his father, who had owned a small farm in Småland but went bankrupt in 1868 and migrated in 1870. After working for another Swedish farmer, the son rented a farm, then moved on to Kansas, and finally settled a homestead in Oklahoma. This pattern of sequential migration was a very common pattern for Swedish migrants to the state at this time, as well as for immigrants generally. Because better agricultural opportunities existed farther west, many of the early Michigan Swedish immigrants who sought land continued on to Wisconsin, Minnesota, and the northern plains states. Those who did not have even the minimal resources needed to homestead first sought wage work and saved their money, relocating later to farming areas.[4]

The period between the Civil War and World War I was a time of massive industrial expansion in the United States. To supply the demand for workers, federal and state governments, as well as private companies such as railroads, actively encouraged European immigration. They established immigration commissions, published pamphlets in many languages, and sent recruiting agents to many countries. Michigan established a Board of Immigration in 1869, and in 1884 the board published a handbook, *Michigan and Its Resources,* which was translated and distributed to immigrant agents in Europe and among the state's existing Swedish population.[5] Many newcomers found that the glowing descriptions and promises of good jobs and high wages produced by these agencies were exaggerated. Those who were considering emigration were more likely to trust the reports of family members and friends, although these were also sometimes inflated by immigrants who wanted to show the folks back home that they had "made good."

Swedes already in the United States encouraged their countrymen to emigrate through a steady stream of letters and visits home which provided information and promised resettlement assistance. In 1883, J. S. Olson, who was living in the area around Gaylord, Michigan, wrote to his brother: "Since I have not yet been long enough at the place I have now moved to, I can't yet determine so well how I have it with the pay, but I am hoping for the best, for when I took the job I was alone without an interpreter and could not understand the conditions." His optimism was based on the experiences of the "21 Swedes [who came] before me, of which half have worked here for several years at the same place and have always been treated fairly, which is not always the case here." Olson had migrated from his natal region with other Swedes who had settled into farming nearby, and now he was offering to help others in turn. He told his brother:

> If Filipsson's hired hand, August Åberg, would like to come to America, tell him or write him that he can well come over in the fall . . . and if he is then in need of money you can give him what he needs out of mine with the agreement that he returns or repays in Swedish money. . . . Besides I will write to Solvalla that I can find him work hereabouts. He can easily repay the journey twice over by spring if he stays healthy. . . . It is very good here, in my opinion, so that I regret I did not come here several years ago.[6]

This pattern of individuals and communities providing encouragement and resources for new immigrants is known as "chain migration" and it is still quite common among many migrant groups.

Swedish immigration remained high until World War I despite several economic downturns, especially the severe depression in the United States during the mid-1890s, peaking between 1900 and 1910. In the early twentieth century, the immigrant population included more industrial workers, a reflection of the rapid but troubled growth of the Swedish industrial sector. Lumbering was an important economic activity, but Sweden was also a major producer of iron, its primary export for many years. In fact, the United States imported Swedish iron ore between 1815 and 1840 until American domestic production began. In Sweden, the quality of the ore varied considerably in different regions, there were insufficient supplies of domestic coal for smelting, and the growing competition from England and other countries (including the United States) negatively affected the industry. Thus many Swedish workers displaced in the lumber and mining sectors were attracted to Michigan, which was actively developing its resource extractive industries at this time.

By the end of the century, as Michigan's economy and communities grew and diversified, urban areas offered new opportunities, especially for talented and entrepreneurial immigrants. Many Swedish migrants were educated and experienced engineers and artisans like carpenters, blacksmiths, and toolsmiths. Most of the later arrivals gravitated toward urban destinations, particularly Chicago, although a significant number settled in Detroit, where many became successful manufacturers and engineers, especially in the early automobile industry. After 1914, World War I severely inhibited European emigration, restrictive U.S. immigration legislation in the 1920s reduced the flood of previous decades to a mere trickle, and the Great Depression of the 1930s took its toll, as did World War II. In addition, social, economic, and political changes in Sweden improved conditions in the twentieth century, making people less inclined to leave.[7]

Three major social institutions defined established Swedish American communities: the church, a wide variety of voluntary associations and clubs, and the press. Local Swedish churches were always at the heart of Swedish American communities because they were stabilizing influences as well as places where homesick immigrants could find social support as well as religious comfort. Tracking the dates of organization of Swedish churches is an excellent way to identify patterns of settlement throughout the state. Similar to the efforts of individuals and families, older communities frequently provided resources and support for the establishment of smaller surrounding settlements. Although it is probably impossible to identify every single Swedish town in Michigan because they are scattered all over the state, clearly there are major clusters in certain areas.

Churches, always the first institution to be organized, often began as small meeting groups in the homes of like-minded congregants. If possible, they raised money to hire a part-time pastor and to rent space until they could buy land and build their own churches. Unfortunately, denominational differences carried over from Sweden sometimes created tensions. Another problem was the isolation of rural communities, which made it hard to attract and to keep regular clergy. Consequently, local religious leaders were often laymen who felt a calling for the ministry, but this practice was controversial. Sunday schools, clubs, choral societies, and other

The Swedish American Churches in America

Swedish churches in the United States were the social bedrock of Swedish American communities, providing crucial support and services, but they could also be sources of contention. Some of these problems carried over from the religious turmoil in Sweden during the nineteenth century, where the dominance of the official Lutheran Church of Sweden was disputed by dissenting religious groups as well as more secular Swedes. In a country with an official ("established") church, everyone must be a member and pay taxes to support the church, even when attendance is not mandatory. In Sweden, everyone had to be baptized in the Lutheran Church or their parents could have been prosecuted. Everyone had to be confirmed and take communion at least once a year in order to enjoy full civil rights, including citizenship, marriage, serving as a witness in court, or even getting a job. Until 1858, worship outside the Church of Sweden was prohibited without special government permission, and dissenters faced prosecution. Prior to the early 1800s, there was not much official repression—partly because the Constitution of 1809 guaranteed religious liberty—but tensions exploded in the early nineteenth century, a period of religious revivalism and dissent from traditional churches in Sweden and many other countries. The Church of Sweden was disestablished in 2000, but remains one of the largest national churches in the world.

A major point of contention derived from Article 14 of the Augsburg (Augustana) Confession, which limited public preaching and administering communion to formally trained clergy. The church feared that if ordinary people began discussing theology, heresy would surely follow. Laws passed as early as 1726 prohibited laymen from preaching in their homes and administering the sacrament. Over time these laws loosened, but Lutheran prejudices against lay preachers (*bond-präster*) persisted and carried over to the American Swedish Lutheran Church. In Sweden, many evangelical believers objected to the organization of the church (which was similar to the Episcopalian tradition) and infant baptism. They advocated the importance of adult conversion experiences, especially for ministers, who were often criticized as too worldly and their services rejected as dry, formalistic, and boring. Dissatisfaction with the official Lutheran clergy led dissenters to rely more on lay preachers and home meetings, which the established church considered heretical and sought to repress. Pastors were powerful but frequently contentious figures. In Sweden they were highly trained, official representatives of the established church responsible for keeping vital statistics and demographic information as well as religious duties. They were elected (by qualified voters), but once installed the pastor was the ultimate authority. In the 1860s the laws began to change. In 1873, dissenters could withdraw from local parish churches if they designated which church they wanted to join, but not until 1908 were they relieved of some of the tax burden for ecclesiastical support. Ironically, the achievement of political alterations that limited the power of the established church disfranchised many lower-class Swedes due to high property qualifications for voting, another motivating factor in Swedish emigration.*

Some Swedish reformers tried to work within the established Church of Sweden by advocating new practices, including training lay practitioners. Many church people accepted that if no regular clergy were available, then lay pastors were adequate as long as they adhered closely to Lutheran doctrine. Those who felt that this compromise was insufficient often left and went to America seeking religious freedom. Thus the Swedish American Lutheran Church was founded by men who were already alienated from the Church of Sweden, sympathetic to pietism and temperance, and determined to establish a different kind of church. Consequently, the Swedish Lutherans considered the American Lutherans to be schismatics and wanted nothing to do with them for many years. In addition, dissenters were also correctly accused of encouraging emigration. Swedish American newspapers were openly hostile toward the Swedish church, and a lot of the immigrant recruitment agents were "free-church" men who appealed to dissident frustrations. Many immigrants remembered being admonished by their local pastors when they went to apply for a permit to emigrate to America, that "Godless land."†

The hostility of the Church of Sweden left Swedish Lutherans in the United States free to structure their church according to their reformist principles, but that did not guarantee internal harmony or prevent other denominations from making gains among Swedish Americans. One of the major tensions immigrated from Sweden with the settlers: traditionalists accepted the Augsburg Confession and its limitations on lay clergy and meetings, while pietists wanted Sunday schools, prayer and revival meetings, and evidence of adult conversion. In 1851,

Swedish Lutherans established the Evangelical Lutheran Synod of Northern Illinois, based on the Augsburg Confession. This group initially included German
and Norwegian congregations, but national and ethnic divisions limited the will-
ingness of Swedes to join with other Lutherans, especially Germans. Traditionalists were upset by the reformist Scandinavians, and vice versa, so in 1860, the
Scandinavian Evangelical Lutheran Augustana Synod was organized; in 1870 the
Norwegians left for nationalistic reasons. The new synod adopted the Augsburg
Confession but also included revivalist elements and accepted lay pastors as
temporary expedients when regular clergy were unavailable. The lack of trained
pastors was a chronic problem, and the Swedish Church was of little help due
to its continuing distrust of an organization full of laymen.

Thus Augustana College was founded in 1860, initially as a theological seminary (now it is a liberal arts college), with instruction in Swedish language and
culture as well as Lutheran doctrine. The Augustana Synod began publishing a
newspaper, *Hemlandet*, in 1855, and later established a publishing company. In
1870, the Augustana Synod had a total membership of 30,000 (of the 200,000
Swedes in the United States); in 1910, about 260,000 of the 1.3 million first-
and second-generation Swedish Americans were affiliated with the Lutheran
Church, with smaller numbers (about 3 percent) associated with other denominations. The Augustana Synod remained separate until 1962 when it merged
with other Scandinavian and German Lutherans to become the Lutheran Church
of America. A subsequent merger with the American Lutheran Church and the
Association of Evangelical Lutheran Churches resulted in the current national
organization, the Evangelical Lutheran Church in America.[‡]

The estrangement between the Swedish and American Lutheran churches
gave other denominations opportunities to gain influence with Swedish people
in America.[§] Over time, Swedish Methodist, Baptist, and Episcopal churches
were established, frequently with the support of their American denominational
counterparts. The Swedish Evangelical Mission Covenant Church was formed
in Stockholm in 1878, and today it is the second largest church in that country.[**]
The church's members, the Mission Friends, thought that even in America traditional Lutheran pastors were too attached to form and structure and were lack-
ing in fundamental faith. Those pastors were, in turn, suspicious of these "free
spirits" who emphasized the "inner call" experienced by a true believer—and

who challenged their authority. The Friends criticized the Lutherans for remaining aloof and doctrinaire and preferred to associate with like-minded persons in other denominations like the Baptists and Methodists. Similar tensions within several American Lutheran synods finally led to the establishment of the Swedish Evangelical Mission Covenant Church in 1885. The church was conservative in doctrine, but welcomed contributions from laypeople, as well as pastors and communicants of other denominations. Over time this church has become more structured, and the hostility between the Friends and the Lutherans has diminished but not disappeared. The Swedish Evangelical Free Church, similar to the Mission Covenant Church in beliefs but differing in church organization, was incorporated in 1908.

Like the Mission Covenant Church, the Methodists and Baptists appealed to more pietistic Swedes. Both these groups were persecuted in Sweden, winning them considerable sympathy; in the United States, most of the Swedish immigrants remained at least nominal Lutherans. The Methodists organized their first Swedish church in the United States four years before the Lutherans, but by 1920 they had only about 21,000 members. In Sweden, similarities between the Episcopal and Lutheran churches had been a major point of contention for the reformists, but these did allow the Church of Sweden to have fairly cordial relations with the American Protestant Episcopal Church. This situation worried American Lutherans, who feared that Swedish Lutherans would encourage immigrants to convert, but the Swedish church grudgingly supported the American Lutherans. Few traditional Lutherans had much reason to become Episcopalians. In 1900, there were only about a dozen Swedish American Episcopalian congregations consisting of approximately two thousand people. Among the Swedes who did become Episcopalians, a class bias was clearly evident. The nonconformism of Baptists, Methodists, and Mission Friends appealed to working-class and rural Swedish Americans, but higher status immigrants were more secular, more anxious to assimilate, and they generally rejected what they perceived as the naive fundamentalism of the masses.[tt]

Swedish churches usually sponsored a number of auxiliary associations, such as groups for women and youth, bands and choirs, and charitable organizations. Large congregations established schools, orphanages, homes for the elderly, and hospitals. Temperance groups attracted many Swedes, although this was also a point of contention between orthodox Lutherans (who tended to avoid the issue) and the nonconformists (who embraced temperance enthusiastically). On a national level, the Salvation Army established a Scandinavian Department (Frälsningsarmén) in 1887. Four Swedish women laundry workers in Brooklyn realized that they were having little luck working among their countrymen with meetings held in English, so they began offering additional Swedish meetings, which soon proved very popular. Approximately eighty branches were eventually established all over the country, usually in cities where there were large Swedish (or Scandinavian) populations. There were Michigan chapters in Escanaba, Gladstone, Muskegon, and Detroit. In Detroit the group was established in 1920 and did well initially, building a large temple in 1930. Due to the repeal of Prohibition and the declining numbers of Swedish speakers, the national Salvation Army finally closed the Swedish Department in 1965.‡‡ In 1902, the Swedish-Finnish Temperance Association was established, later merging with the Swedish-Finnish Benevolent Association to become the International Order of Runeberg. A Detroit Lodge #29 was organized in 1926.§§

Temperance activism had a distinctly religious component, but many of the other organizations established by Swedes in the United States were con-

affiliated groups were popular, and holidays were times for traditional celebrations. For many decades, services were usually held in Swedish, but in the 1930s most churches shifted to English in an attempt to appeal to younger generations of Swedish Americans, or to supplement declining membership by including people of other ethnic groups. In the twentieth century, assimilation and secularization affected church membership and sometimes led to mergers with other (usually Scandinavian) congregations, but many Swedish American churches are still in existence and remain proud of their histories.

Part of the declining influence of the churches was due to the growth in voluntary associations, secular societies, and clubs. Like many immigrant groups, Swedes were very active in the establishment of lodges, benevolent associations, women's groups, music societies, and many other social, cultural, and educational organizations which offered collegiality, educational demned by Swedish ministers because of their secular character. A greater threat to the Swedish churches was the increasing numbers of second-generation Swedish Americans who lacked connections to the parent country and fluency in the language. The formation of church-associated groups was one attempt to broaden the membership base, and merging congregations was another. Most Swedish churches found it necessary to switch to English services in the 1920s and 1930s, and in the twenty-first century only a few still hold special services in Swedish, such as the Christmas Julotta service. Many of these churches still exist, however, and though they have lost much of their distinctively Swedish identity, they are well aware of their histories—frequently documented in centennial or other publications and celebrations—and of their tremendous significance in the history of Swedish people in America.

* Florence E. Janson, *The Background of Swedish Immigration* (Chicago: University of Illinois Press, 1931), 167–221; George M. Stephenson, *The Religious Aspects of Swedish Immigration: A Study of Immigrant Churches* (Minneapolis: University of Minnesota Press, 1932), 2–7, 143–144.
† Stephenson, *The Religious Aspects of Swedish Immigration*, 47–89, 133–141.
‡ Ibid., 147–244.
§ Ibid., 12–25.
** Ibid., 103–109.
†† Ibid., 200–263, 278–288.
‡‡ Edward O. Nelson, "Recollections of the Salvation Army's Scandinavian Corps," *Swedish American Historical Quarterly* 29:4 (Oct. 1978): 257–276.
§§ Christian T. Feddersen, *Scandinavians in Michigan* (Hancock, Michigan: The Book Concern, 1968), 262–263.

and cultural opportunities, and social status. The various groups also offered an organizational alternative for those "free-thinkers" who objected to the powerful influence of religion and local churches. They frequently drew the hostility of the Swedish clergy, which condemned them for precisely this reason, as well as for the secular activities these groups sponsored—especially "questionable" entertainments like dances. There was also a distinct class element involved. The early Swedish immigrants were not usually wealthy or well educated, they were often deeply religious, and they came from isolated rural areas which were not well integrated as part of a "national" culture. Later immigrants were often better educated, frequently urban workers, many of whom became economically successful in the United States. They tended to reject what they considered frontier fundamentalism and rural ways, and were eager to assimilate and adopt the ways of middle-class American life. Membership in these societies soon became a badge of socioeconomic

Zion Lutheran Church, Skanee, Michigan, 2010. Photograph by author.

status and success.[8] Swedish-speaking Finns usually preferred to have their own benevolent and cultural associations. Nationally the Swedish-Finnish Benevolent Aid Association was first organized in 1900.

At their peak in 1910, Swedish American organizations had at least 100,000 adult members, while the Swedish American churches had about 365,000 members. Thus approximately half of the Swedish American population was affiliated with a Swedish ethnic organization of one type or another. Nationally, several different organizations were formed by Swedish Americans. The Svea Society, established in Chicago in 1857, became the prototype for other groups. Another important group was the Vasa Order, named for King Gustav I (Gustavas Vasa), which was established in New England in the 1890s and is still in existence. Originally a benevolent association, the Vasa Order eventually became the largest such organization in the country—by 1928 it had seventy-two thousand members in more than four hundred lodges. Over the years, its members also became involved in efforts to preserve Swedish culture.[9]

The earliest secular societies were usually benevolent societies, which gave concrete assistance in times of trouble by providing advantages such as sickness or death benefits and funeral expenses. Over time, many of these organizations expanded to provide libraries (with Swedish and Swedish American newspapers), theatrical entertainments, and other social events. Sometimes they were large enough to own their own buildings and halls large enough to host community gatherings.

After 1900 these groups were often concerned with the preservation of Swedish language and culture in the United States. By the 1890s, Swedes began to celebrate their rich cultural heritage, both in America and in

Church group in front of Swedish Evangelical Lutheran Messiah Church, Marquette, Michigan, ca. 1915. Courtesy Marquette County History Museum.

Sweden. Swedish Americans argued that one could be a loyal American citizen, well assimilated into the dominant culture, and still take pride in one's ethnic identity. According to many sources, Swedish Americans often assimilated rapidly into American culture, and many enjoyed considerable upward social and economic mobility, at least in some areas. This was particularly true of arrivals after 1900. More likely to be literate urbanites than earlier immigrants, they tended to learn English quickly and had high rates of public school attendance, naturalization, and home ownership. One exception was in marriage patterns: Swedes were the least likely of the Northern Europeans to marry outside their group, and when they did, it was usually with other Scandinavians.[10]

Ironically, while they quickly adapted to American middle-class culture, they also became more conscious of their "Swedishness." They began what has been described as a "conscious effort to create a distinctive identity by an immigrant group now assured of its place in American society." Early twentieth-century Swedish Americans were more likely to have been exposed to the influences of Swedish national cultural revivalism as it developed in the late nineteenth century. As a result, they began to establish a number of community cultural organizations partly to preserve the language and customs of the homeland, and in the twenty-first century they still serve this function. Many of the cultural traditions they "preserved" were in fact "invented" or at least modified to suit new needs. For example, the St. Lucia festival on December 13 was not widely celebrated in Sweden except among the more fortunate.[11]

Another important influence was the Swedish language newspaper, which reflected many of the trends discussed above. While many of the early settlers were not well educated, they were usually literate (although not in English). They appreciated a Swedish language newspaper because they were anxious for resources to supplement their limited educational opportunities, interested in current events and community news both in America and in Sweden, and eager to learn about the new ways of life in America. According to some estimates, there were as many as 1,500 Swedish American publications between 1855 and 1910 in twenty-nine states. Given that they frequently went out of business or changed names a more accurate estimate is probably about 650, and many of these were quite small.

The first Swedish papers originated in the major population centers of

Chicago and New York, as publications sponsored by religious organizations, such as the Augustana Synod–affiliated paper, *Hemlandet (The Homeland)*, established in 1855. This paper, like other influential Swedish language periodicals that were established over the subsequent years, was published in Chicago. In the early twentieth century, many of these publications began to falter. In 1914, two influential periodicals, the *Svenska Amerikanaren* and *Svenska Tribunen* merged, boosting circulation to seventy-six thousand readers, but these numbers soon began to decline due to the growing problems of maintaining a separate ethnic press. The interruption in immigration, growing anti-immigrant sentiment, and government censorship during World War I were serious blows—and the fact that some Swedes expressed pro-German sentiments certainly did not help. After the 1920s, the audience for these papers shrank rapidly because immigration from Sweden declined dramatically due to new U.S. immigration restrictions, the Great Depression, and World War II, and because conditions in Sweden were improving, reducing the incentive to move.[12]

The papers declined as the composition and interests of the Swedish American population shifted over the decades of the twentieth century. Since their audience was largely foreign-born Swedes—people who still retained close ties to their home countries and who were fluent in the language—the papers did not appeal to subsequent generations of assimilated Swedish Americans who lacked the capacity to communicate in Swedish. The newspaper publishers debated how to address this problem, but found no successful resolution. As a result, there were seventy-three Swedish papers in seventeen different states claiming a total of 560,000 readers in 1915, but by 1932 only thirty-five weeklies or monthlies were left. By 1940 this number had dropped to twenty, and as of 2000, there were only four left: *Veskusten, California Veckoblad, Svenska Amerikanaren Tribunen* (all in California), and *Nordstjernan* (in New York City), which survived with the help of subsidies by the Swedish government.[13]

According to one source, between 1880 and 1938 there were approximately forty-five Swedish language newspapers printed in Michigan. (They are sometimes difficult to trace because many failed after a few years and changed names and publishers on a regular basis.) In lower Michigan there were Swedish newspapers in Battle Creek (where most were religious publications connected to the Seventh Day Adventists), Cadillac, Detroit,

Finnish Swedes and Swedish Finns:
Early Internationalists

The histories of Swedes and Finns have been intertwined for many centuries. There are still distinct groups of both Finnish-speaking Swedes and Swedish-speaking Finns in Scandinavia and the United States, the result of specific historical circumstances and migration patterns throughout the Baltic region and in America.

Swedes in Finland

Sweden controlled what is now Finland for more than six hundred years. Swedish migration into the Baltic area began in the 1300s, partly due to overpopulation, but it also was apparently motivated by the desire to extend Christianity. Thus this relocation was encouraged by the Swedish church and royal authorities, both of which sought to expand and to consolidate their influence in Finland. Scholars disagree whether in these areas there were already Finns who subsequently became Swedish speakers, or whether the Swedes moved into largely uninhabited regions. Over time, however, communities of Swedish-speaking and Finnish-speaking fishermen and peasants in the Gulf of Bothnia began to share similar Finnish cultural characteristics. Today the main Swedish-speaking areas of Finland are Åboland, Åland, Österbotten, and Nyland.

During the sixteenth and seventeenth centuries, the Swedish Empire expanded to encompass the present-day regions of Estonia, Latvia, Lithuania, and Northern Germany, but it began to decline in the eighteenth century, largely as a result of competition with Russia. In 1807, Czar Alexander I and Napoleon decided that Finland should become part of Russia. The Swedish monarch, King Gustav IV, was an implacable foe of Napoleon, but he failed to take measures to defend Finland even when it became clear that the Russians were mobilizing an invasion force. Humiliating Swedish losses in the subsequent war led to Gustav's deposition from the throne and the establishment of the Russian Grand Duchy of Finland in 1809. At that time, approximately 15 percent of the Finnish population spoke Swedish (currently Swedish speakers represent about 6 percent of the population). Swedish was the language of the educated elite, the schools, and government administration, but in the nineteenth century, urbanization and migration brought more Finnish speakers into the predominantly Swedish-speaking cities and accelerated the use of Finnish. After 1809, Russian authorities promoted a revival of Finnish culture and language in order to diminish Swedish influence in the country and to deter any reunification efforts. In 1863 Czar Alexander II officially established bilingualism, which was confirmed by the Finnish constitution of 1919 and remains the official policy today. These developments caused mixed feelings among the Swedish-speaking Finns. Some enthusiastically supported the shift toward Finnish nationalism, while others feared "Russification," or the absorption of Finnish into Russian cultural nationalism. Those who were not willing to re-identify as Finnish nationals moved back to Sweden or emigrated abroad, so Finnish gradually became the dominant language. Today many Swedish Finns consider themselves Finns, but identify themselves as a separate ethnic group. Fifty percent still live in areas where Swedish is the dominant language, but for all practical purposes they are functionally bilingual.*

Finns in Sweden

Communities of Finns living in what is now Sweden can be traced back to the beginning of the fourteenth century. Their settlements centered around the northern end of the Gulf of Bothnia and near the Torne River Valley (which currently forms part of the border between the two countries). In 1523, a Swedish nobleman, Gustav Vasa, became King Gustav I after he led a successful rebellion that liberated Sweden from Danish dominance. In the following decades, Gustav I and his successors (Charles IX and Gustav II Adolphus) encouraged Finnish immigration to develop agriculture in the underpopulated areas of Dalarna (Dalecarlia) and the eastern part of Värmland (Bergslagen) in central Sweden. These were the *skogsfinnar,* or "forest Finns" of the Finnskogar (Finn woods). For several decades they were left alone to hunt elk and to practice their methods of slash-and-burn farming, but when iron deposits were discovered in the area, Swedish-speaking Swedes began to move in and before long trouble began between the two groups. Accused of wasteful deforestation and overhunting elk, the Finns resisted measures designed to curb these practices. Finally, in 1637 the Finns who could not prove that they held title to their lands were ordered to leave Sweden. Conveniently, at this time Swedish settlers were needed for the new colony in America, so the Finns were encouraged to emigrate. Few volunteered, however, because they were reluctant to leave their homes and they distrusted Swedish assurances that they would be left alone in their new homes. So the Swedish government used coercive measures, issuing order to "capture the forest destroyers and ship them west." As a result, the "troublemakers" were arrested and transported to the new colony on the Delaware River.[†]

In Sweden, fear of Russian influences after 1809 led the Swedish government to repress the Finnish language and to assimilate the Finnish Swedes. As a result, many left, while those who stayed were mostly clustered around the northern border with Finland. Further migration from Finland to Sweden occurred in the years before and after World War II, but many of these people were Swedish-speaking Finns. Assimilationist policies were reversed in the 1970s, and Finnish is now one of five official minority languages in Sweden.[‡]

Finns and Swedes in America

Many of the early Swedish settlers in North America were both Finnish-speaking Swedes and Swedish-speaking Finns. As described above, the former were among the earliest arrivals in New Sweden, settling in a number of communities with distinctly Finnish names (e.g., Finland, Upland, and Takamaa or Tacony, now Philadelphia). Even after Sweden stopped reinforcing the colony and it was lost, first to the Dutch and then to the English, Swedish Finns continued to immigrate. These people were well prepared for life on the frontier. One of their enduring contributions was the log cabin, used as both home and bath house (sauna), a structural form quickly adopted by other immigrant groups.[§]

Most of the Swedish-speaking Finns who migrated to the United States and to Michigan in the nineteenth century came from the Österbotten area, but oth-

Grand Rapids (eleven between 1888 and 1903), Ludington, Manistee, and Muskegon (five). In the Upper Peninsula there were Swedish publications in Calumet, Escanaba, Iron Mountain, Ironwood, Ishpeming (six between 1887–1918), and Manistique. Some were religious journals, while others were secular. If politically oriented, they aligned with the Republican Party, which the majority of Swedes tended to support in the years between the Civil War

ers were from the Åland Islands, Åbo, and Nyland. Before the 1870s, the small numbers are hard to locate, but one area of concentration was in Ludington, Michigan. In the mid-1880s many were attracted to the forests and mills of Michigan's Lower Peninsula. As the timber was cut down, the immigrants moved north and west following the logging industry, settling in the Upper Peninsula of Michigan as well as the northern areas of Wisconsin and Minnesota. Swedish Finns in the Upper Peninsula were also fishers along the lakeshore and miners, mainly in the western iron ranges.** They still identify themselves as distinct from the larger Swedish American population, although the differences are often lost on others. While there are some lingering tensions and prejudices between the Swedish- and Finnish-speaking Finns—Swedish-speakers being perceived as elitist imperialists and Finnish-speakers as poor backcountry folk—the shared experience of immigration has helped diminish these stereotypes over time. As one Crystal Falls woman originally from the Åland Islands recalled, "We never had anything to do with the Finns in Old Country. Their officials had to speak Swedish. It was a dishonor to talk with them. Russia had stolen Åland from Sweden and given it to Finland, you see. Then when we came over here and lived with them, we found they were as good people as we were."††

* "Swedish-speaking Finns," Wikipedia, The Free Encyclopedia, http://en.wikipedia.org/w/index.php?title=Swedish-speaking_Finns&oldid=304771692.
† Christopher Ward, The Dutch and Swedes on the Delaware (Philadelphia: University of Pennsylvania Press, 1930), 102–104; Amandus Johnson, The Swedish Settlements on the Delaware, 1638-1664, vol. 2 (New York: D. Appleton & Company, 1927), 634.
‡ "Sweden Finns," Wikipedia, The Free Encyclopedia, http://en.wikipedia.org/w/index.php?title=Sweden_Finns&oldid=302450860.
§ For a complete history of Swedish colonization experiences in America, see Ward, The Dutch and Swedes, and Johnson, The Swedish Settlements on the Delaware, vols. 1 and 2.
** Anders Myhrman, "The Finland-Swedes in America," Swedish American Historical Quarterly 31:1 (Jan. 1980): 16–33; Anders Myhrman, Finlandssvenskar I Amerika: The Finland Swedes in America (Helsingfors, Finland: Svenska Litteratursällskapet i Finland, 1973); Armas K. E. Holmio, History of the Finns in Michigan, trans. Ellen M. Ryynanen (Detroit: Wayne State University Press, 2001), 405–412; Jeffrey W. Hancks, Scandinavians in Michigan (East Lansing: Michigan State University Press, 2006), 33–35.
†† Richard M. Dorson, Bloodstoppers and Bearwalkers: Folk Tales of Canadians, Lumberjacks, and Indians (Cambridge: Harvard University Press, 1972), 10.

and the Great Depression due to the party's opposition to antislavery and its support for homesteading, industrialization, and open immigration. There were Swedish socialists, too, but they were usually not particularly radical in their support for small farmers and industrial workers. Like the churches, the newspapers can be used a rough guide to patterns of Swedish settlement throughout the state.[14]

Eleventh Annual Swedish-Finnish Temperance Association of America Convention, Dollar Bay, Michigan, 1913. Courtesy Superior View.

Immigrant papers contained a variety of reports and news of both the old and new countries. Most of the content was regional, not national, because readers wanted information about their home areas and people they knew, resulting in many apparently insignificant, even gossipy stories. The editors and writers of these papers—who were usually educated urbanites before migration and "immigrant intellectuals" afterward—often complained of their readers' lack of interest in more exalted subjects (such as literature and politics), their materialism, and their preference for sensational and violent news—accidents, fires, and crime. Even though they had to "give the readers what they want" in order to sell papers, the publishers realized that the immigrants valued their educational functions as well. The periodicals did contain serialized stories, poems, humor, and other cultural features. Their role in helping new immigrants understand the American political system was invaluable. However, the treatment of politics was sometimes questionable, particularly when suspicions arose that there was a payoff behind editorial endorsement for a particular candidate. The papers were chronically desperate for money, relying on advertisements for most of their income. The ads give a very good picture of ethnic business communities, but these were declining, too, as assimilation progressed over the decades. In many ways, the letters and submissions by readers are of most lasting interest to historians, genealogists, and other students of Swedish American culture.[15]

In summary, Swedish immigration and settlement in Michigan reflected many of these general trends. Furthermore, there were several clearly distinct phases of Swedish migration and settlement in the state, which are discussed in the following chapters. Immigration in the years just before and after the Civil War, when Swedes settled largely in lower Michigan, is the subject of the first chapter. Swedes tended to cluster in the western region of the state near Lake Michigan where there were jobs in the lumber and railroad industries as well as land for farming. During the period of massive immigration in the 1880s, the migrants usually headed to the Upper Peninsula, as discussed in the second chapter. By the early twentieth century, urban development and manufacturing attracted many Swedes to the growing cities, particularly Detroit. This is the topic of the third chapter, which concludes with a brief discussion of the Swedish American presence in Michigan today.

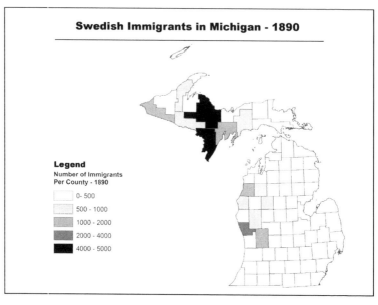

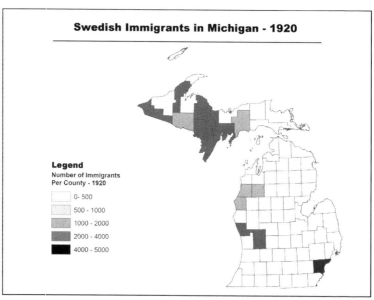

Swedish Populations of Michigan, 1890 and 1920. Maps prepared by Cameron Feuss, Northern Michigan University.

Early Migration and Settlement in Lower Michigan

ery few Swedes came to Michigan before the Civil War. According to the U.S. Census, there were only sixteen in 1850 and fewer than three hundred by 1860. Many of the earliest Swedish immigrants sought better farming land further west, or they settled in cities such as Chicago and Minneapolis where there were already established ethnic communities. There were very few Swedes in Detroit until the early twentieth century, however. When Swedes began to arrive in Michigan in greater numbers after 1860, they gravitated to the western part of the state near Lake Michigan. Along the coast, there were concentrations of Swedes in the counties of Manistee, Mason, Oceana, Muskegon, Ottawa, and Berrien. A bit inland, significant numbers of Swedes settled in Wexford, Mecosta, Osceola, Newaygo, and Kent counties. In these areas, some farming was possible, but the growth industries were lumbering and railroad construction. In the forests along the coast, cut timber was floated down the rivers and lakes to sawmills and processing centers in Manistee, Muskegon, and especially Grand Rapids. Similar circumstances also attracted settlers to the Saginaw region in eastern Michigan, particularly around Bay City. These early residents were usually small clusters of several families who migrated then settled together or groups of young men working in the lumber industry.[16]

In 1860, eight counties had ten or more Swedish-born residents: Kent (with sixty Swedes living in Sparta and Kent), Muskegon (forty-one in Muskegon, Oceana, and Dalton), St. Clair (thirty-four in China), Mason (sixteen in Little Sauble), Wayne (sixteen in Detroit), Washtenaw (fifteen in Salem), Manistee (fourteen in Manistee), Manitou (eleven on North Manitou Island), and Macomb (ten in Chesterfield). By 1870, many of these towns had grown considerably and new ones had been established: near Lake Michigan, 117 Swedish-born residents lived in Sparta, 106 in Whitehall, ninety-one in Muskegon, eighty-nine in Manistee, and forty in Grand Rapids. Other new settlements included the towns of Newberg (Cass County), with twenty-nine Swedish-born inhabitants, Pere Marquette (Mason County), with seventy, and Laketon (Muskegon County), with twenty-five Swedish residents.

Most of the new immigrants lacked the capital to purchase land initially, so men often worked for wages part of the year as they saved their money. Some bought land and then spent their weekends and summers—sometimes for years—improving their properties. Swedish agrarians were largely self-sufficient: the men were skilled carpenters and smiths, making and repairing most of their own implements, while the women were traditionally responsible for dairying and the care of cattle, as well as textile production. Swedish American women frequently contributed to the family economy by providing surplus products like eggs, milk, or butter to local consumers. In both Sweden and America, young women frequently went out to work, either in the fields along with men or as domestic servants in private homes or local boarding houses. Displaced by the agrarian crisis Sweden experienced in the middle of the nineteenth century, these young people were eager to emigrate in search of better jobs and potential marriage partners.

The first major concentration of Swedish Americans was located in Kent County, where a small group settled in 1853. Many of them were from Småland, in southern Sweden. After a difficult journey, they landed in Boston, lived in Plymouth, Michigan (Wayne County) for three years, then moved on to establish the Kent County communities of Alpine, Kent City (formerly Lisbon), and Sparta, where later they were joined by additional groups of Swedish immigrants. Many of these people were very poor and they were probably attracted to the area by the knowledge that fellow Swedes were already settled there. Sometimes the men came first, leaving their families behind in Sweden or Chicago as they cleared land for small farms. In 1860, there were nine or ten families in Kent County; by 1870, there were almost

Toger Johnson at his farm, Newberry, Michigan, ca. 1890. Courtesy Superior View.

two hundred Swedes living in the county; by 1880, Kent County had more than five hundred Swedish inhabitants.

At first the nearest facilities were in Grand Rapids, about twenty miles away from Kent City, but soon the town got its own sawmill and grist mill. In 1859, a visiting minister reported that the Swedes of Kent City had built a school, and in 1866, the first Swedish Evangelical Lutheran church in Michigan, the Swedish Evangelical Lutheran Mamrelund Congregation, was organized. In the summer of 1872 they built a church. One of these founders, John Johnson, had no musical training, but he built an organ for the church and played it for the next thirty-five years. The son of one of the early pioneers in Kent County, Charles Theodore Gan (or Grawn), was president of Central Michigan Normal School (now Central Michigan University) from 1900–1918, and one of his grandsons, William Grawn Milliken, became the governor of Michigan in 1969. Charles Herbert Blomstrom, who later established the C. H. Blomstrom Motor Company in Detroit, was also born in Kent City.[17]

Another important site of early Swedish settlement was Osceola County, particularly the town of Tustin (originally New Bleking). The Swedish population of four in 1870 increased rapidly to 398 in 1880, and by 1890 the population peaked at 643 before beginning to decline. Initially, immigration to the area had been slow (perhaps because it gained a reputation as a country of marshes and dry unproductive areas), but the railroad companies needed labor, and Scandinavians were favored because they were considered to be sober and hard workers. Combining assets to form the Continental Improvement Company, four regional lines advertised in the Swedish press, and they also hired the Reverend Josiah P. Tustin of St. Mark's Episcopal Church in Grand Rapids to return to Sweden and recruit settlers. Rev. Tustin was engaged in an effort to improve relations between the (Lutheran) Church of Sweden and the U.S. Episcopal Church, and while he did not accomplish this goal, he did succeed in his recruitment efforts. Tustin made several trips and attracted more than one thousand Swedes to Grand Rapids (Kent County), Osceola County, Newaygo County, Mecosta County, and Wexford County. After helping the immigrants get settled, Tustin moved on to Wisconsin; the town of New Bleking was renamed in his honor in 1872.

Although emigrants had to pay their own way across the ocean, the railroad consortium offered free transportation to Michigan from New York, housing assistance, good wages ($1.75 to $2.00 per day), and the newcomers were not required to promise to stay. The biggest attraction was the opportunity to buy land. The railroads owned more than a million acres which could be purchased for $5 per acre (on credit), and government land was also available at $2.50 per acre. The focal point of settlement was the town of New Bleking, built on forty acres of land donated by the Grand Rapids and Indiana Railroad. The first church in Tustin was organized in 1872. It was an Episcopalian church, undoubtedly due to Rev. Tustin's influence, but since most of the settlers were orthodox Lutherans, they soon decided to form their own congregation, the Swedish Evangelical Church, in April 1874. By the late 1870s, Tustin was an established community, with a hotel, a newspaper (the *Tustin Herald*), and a permanent Lutheran pastor, John Forsberg—who was also a local machinist, blacksmith, and missionary.

Forsberg's combination of talents was not unusual for a rural Swedish minister in America. Forsberg came to the United States in 1866, spent several years working his trade and traveling on missionary work, then decided to acquire formal seminary training in 1877. While in Tustin he organized churches at Reed City, Cadillac, Hobart, Morley, and Bound's Mill. One of Forsberg's neighbors, Andrew Dahlstrom, was a former cabinetmaker from Chicago who bought land and became a farmer and the pastor of the Swedish Free Church. In the United States, rural isolation, small congregations, and the lack of trained ministers meant men of faith like Forsberg and Dahlstrom often served their communities in multiple capacities. They were sometimes subjected to harassment and derision because of their unofficial status, however, which was probably a factor in Forsberg's decision to seek seminary training and ordination.[18]

One of Sparta's early residents, Godfrey J. Anderson (born in 1895), moved in and out of the area with his family several times, undoubtedly seeking better economic conditions. After serving in the U.S. Army, Anderson returned to work in the Grand Rapids furniture industry until his retirement. In later life he described the importance of the Swedish Evangelical [Mission] Church in providing community cohesion and some relief to the monotony of farm life, especially at Christmas. Even then, "for the most part there was something dull, lonely and forlorn about Christmas Day in the country," but everyone bustled about preparing lots of good food for both the annual Sunday school Yulefest, followed by the Julotta service at church.[19] The holiday season offered a chance to visit with neighbors, drink lots of coffee, and eat delicious dishes such as *lutefisk,* Christmas *korv* (sausage), *calva dans* (a custard-like dish made from new raw milk), and all kinds of pastries and baked goods. The Sunday school gathering, which was held at one of the local farms, could be somewhat tedious for young people since it involved scripture readings and speeches by the pastor and others, and it could also be a bit intimidating for those called upon to give recitations. To brighten things up there was music and hymn singing, the lighting of the tree, presents, and more food and coffee before everyone packed back into their wagons and sleighs and headed home.[20]

The Julotta service was even more important, as everyone got up in the wee hours of the morning, and "set out for church carrying a torch or lantern and singing carols along the way." Anderson recalled, "The whole countryside was alive with bobbing, flickering lights, and the sounds of sleighbells, merry greetings and singing were wafting from afar on the frosty morning air." The sanctuary was full of lighted candles, greenery, and the singing of traditional hymns. Christmas Day was a relatively quiet family day, but the

second day of Christmas, St. Stephen's Day, was devoted to more carol singing and neighborhood visiting, and so it continued throughout the Christmas
season. Anderson reports that "King Canute, who ruled Sweden a thousand
years ago, wisely decreed that the season should end on Saint Hillary's Day,
the 20th of Jan; otherwise the Swedes, in their exuberance, most likely would
have celebrated Christmas all winter." These celebrations were extremely
important to Swedish people in America, allowing them to maintain contact
with their original homeland and to perpetuate old traditions in their new
home.[21]

   As railroad construction and logging expanded throughout Michigan in
the 1870s, Swedish settlements also grew. Due to the efforts of Rev. Forsberg
and others, Swedish Lutheran churches were established in the nearby
communities of Hobart, Gilbert, Jennings, and LeRoy. Some of these towns
were too small to support an exclusively Swedish church, however, so Scandinavian Lutherans often organized together initially or combined later. In
Big Rapids (Mecosta County), Immanuel Lutheran Church was established
when local Swedish and Danish congregations merged; the northeast side
of town where the church was located was called "Swede Hill." Cadillac,
in Wexford County, had four Swedish churches and a Swedish newspaper.
The original Zion Lutheran Church was established in 1874 and led by Rev.
Forsberg from 1877 to 1883. Other Swedish churches in Cadillac included the
Swedish Christian Mission Church (established in 1880), the Free Methodist Church (1881), and the Swedish Baptist Church (1883). The community
also supported the Gotha Society, a mutual aid and fraternal group, which
constructed a building now used by the American Legion.

   In Manistee (Manistee County), due west of Cadillac on the Lake Michigan coast, Our Savior's Historical Museum Church is the former Our Savior's
Evangelical Lutheran Church. Built in 1870, and now listed on the National
Historic Register, it was officially a Danish church, but Swedes helped build it
and attended services there until they formed their own church, the Swedish
Messiah Lutheran Church. One of the prominent local Swedish inhabitants
of Manistee was Lewis Larsson (more commonly known as Louis Sands). He
started as a lumberjack, bought forest land, and built his own sawmill in the
1870s. Sands diversified his activities—earning himself the name the "Salt
King" for the salt works he established in 1886—and became a millionaire,
the leading employer in Manistee, and a major civic donor.[22]

Some of these communities, such as White Cloud (Newaygo County), Big Rapids (Mecosta County), and Bailey (Muskegon County) were heavily settled by Swedish Finns. These folks also immigrated into eastern Michigan around the Bay City, Oscoda, and East Tawas areas to work in the forests and sawmills. Those who settled in western Michigan around Ludington and Muskegon were attracted to fishing as well as lumbering, and they often stayed after the timber was cut and the mills closed. In Ludington, Swedish immigrants established Emanuel Swedish Lutheran Church in 1874, which grew to be one of the largest Swedish churches in lower Michigan, and also a Free Mission church and a Baptist church.[23] People in the smaller communities adapted as best they could when the lumber was depleted in the Lower Peninsula and the timber industry moved north into the Upper Peninsula. In the twentieth century many moved to Flint and to Detroit to work in the automobile industry. In White Cloud, Matt and Hilma Gust operated "Swede's Saloon" until Prohibition, and then they went into the hotel business. The Swedish Mission Church in White Cloud was organized in 1908 but closed in 1966 as older members passed away and their children lost interest or left town seeking better economic opportunities.[24]

South of Grand Rapids, the first Swedish settlers in Allegan County arrived at Abronia (just south of Allegan) in 1867, where they were subsequently joined by other groups in the 1870s. When Swedish Lutherans decided to organize a church in 1878, they asked the Lisbon (now Kent City) minister to help them, establishing the Swedish Lutheran Sandhem Church of Abronia (later Immanuel Lutheran Church). In St. Joseph (Berrien County), there were only two Swedish inhabitants in 1860 (but 112 by 1870), located primarily in the towns of Benton, Lincoln, Niles, and especially St. Joseph, which had a Swedish-born population of forty-seven that year. Because the Scandinavian population was not large, Swedish, Danish, and Norwegian Lutherans joined together to establish the Saron Lutheran Church in 1875. Initially the small congregation was served by visiting pastors and it met in the fire hall. In 1882, the congregation purchased and remodeled a building that previously had housed a rescue mission and a roller skating rink. Soon thereafter they acquired a full-time pastor. Because services were in Swedish, the church did not expand until a new minister arrived in 1918 and shifted to English. As a result, the church began to attract new members, outgrew its original home, and built a new structure in 1927. It remains an important community institution, as do many of the Swedish churches, despite the dilution of their original ethnic identities.[25]

Consistent with the regional pattern of growth and decline associated with the lumber business, the Swedish-born population of Muskegon County increased rapidly in the 1870s and 1880s and reached a peak of 2,442 in 1890. From 1870 to 1900, the Whitehall area, located just north of Muskegon at the mouth of the White River, was the largest lumbering center on the Lake Michigan shoreline. It was a flourishing community with as many as seventeen sawmills at one time, and later a large tannery was established. The first Swedish settler was Charles Johnson, who arrived in 1866 and encouraged many of his countrymen to join him. At first, almost all of them were young men who went to work in the lumber camps or for the Grand Rapids and Indiana Railroad. In 1870, roughly 70 percent of the town's one thousand inhabitants were Swedes living in an area still known as "Swedentown." Most of them were employed in the sawmills, but some were hotel keepers, store keepers, and saloon keepers as well as farmers. In 1868 the Scandinavian Lutheran Church was organized, followed by the Swedish Evangelical Lutheran Lebanon Church in 1872, the First Swedish Lutheran Church in 1875, and a Mission Friends [Covenant] church in 1881. The Lakeside Baptist Church was founded by Swedes who first joined the local Baptists, but then decided to establish their own congregation, the Elim Swedish Baptist Church, in 1881. There was a Swedish Hall, a Swedish newspaper (which changed its name several times), and a Swedish Society Norden—a mutual benefit society founded in 1879 and still in existence in 1913.[26]

A lengthy autobiography written by a longtime Swedish American resident of Muskegon, Frederick Nelson, is virtually a minihistory of the Swedish experience in this area. Encouraged by a visiting friend of his parents already living in Muskegon, Nelson emigrated in 1903 at the age of twenty. Accompanied by his two younger sisters, he joined a party of seventeen young emigrant Swedes. After his arrival in Michigan, Nelson lived on a local farm with another friend of his parents until he found work in town, while his sisters took jobs in service to American families. Unable to find good jobs due to his lack of English language skills, Nelson soon accepted an offer to head "up north" to work for a lumbering operation which offered good wages, despite the warning of the local pastor that, "You are too nice a young man to leave for an unknown place to you, and live with lumberjacks, where there are no churches." As Christmas approached, the heavy snow reminded Nelson of Sweden and he grew nostalgic and lonely for his family. On Christmas Eve, Nelson was dismayed when the men got drunk and started to fight, almost kicking over the stove and starting a fire. The next morning, however, he convinced them all to attend services provided by a traveling minister. Although Nelson did not understand much of the sermon because of his poor English, he was impressed by the sight of "my comrades, these hard working woodsmen, sitting there so quietly, listening, many of them with tears in their eyes." Later he wrote to his worried pastor in Muskegon, telling him about this experience.[27]

For five years, Nelson moved back and forth between Muskegon and the northern woods. He enjoyed the social, cultural, and intellectual opportunities provided by the urban Swedish American community, and he was able to find work in local woodworking factories, but better wages drew him back to lumbering. He finally decided to settle permanently in Muskegon for two reasons. First, economic opportunities were changing: "New factories were moving into Muskegon, as the great sawmill era was gradually dying out," Nelson said. Second, his parents and two additional siblings arrived from Sweden in 1906 and he wanted to be closer to his family and to help them with their new farm. The family lived and worked in town for many months, clearing land and building a house during weekends and summers. In 1908, Nelson married a Swedish girl from Chicago—a friend of one of his sisters—and settled down, although he continued to work in town and on his parents' farm. Through hard work and careful household management, the Nelsons were soon able to buy land of their own, and eventually build both a house in town and one on the farm. Nelson's wife, Hannah, was not keen on rural life, but their farm supported them during the Depression after Nelson lost his job. As an established member of the community, he contributed to various Swedish (and later English) publications and local political debates and was active in local Swedish lodges and the Swedish Mission Church. In his later years he traveled extensively with his wife, including trips back to Sweden. His colorful autobiography describes a life of hard work and achievement which was typical of so many Swedish immigrants.[28]

Once the railroads were completed and the timber was exhausted in the early 1890s, many of the small communities dependent upon these activities dwindled or died. Survival required new, more diversified economic strategies. Some Swedes shifted to farming, while others continued to service the railroads, but many gravitated to the regional centers of Muskegon and Grand Rapids. Because these were centralized locations near Lake Michigan, they soon became the largest communities in the area, but from 1890 to 1900, times were hard due to a national economic depression and the closure or relocation of the local sawmills. Yet as Nelson described, he was able to remain in Muskegon because its economic focus shifted to machine shops, foundries, and other forms of manufacturing after 1900. For example, in 1911 Charles E. Johnson, the inventor of the automobile piston ring, founded the Piston Ring Company—later the Sealed Power Corporation—in Muskegon.

Grand Rapids, the largest city in western Michigan, became a major center for furniture production. It attracted Swedes partly because it was located near many of the earliest Swedish settlements in the area, and partly because many Swedes were skilled carpenters and woodworkers. The first Swedish inhabitant, Claus Hokanson, arrived in 1865, and five years later there were fewer than one hundred Swedes, but the numbers increased rapidly. In 1910, there were 929 foreign-born Swedes living in the city, in addition to 919 second-generation Swedish Americans. By 1920, these numbers increased to 2,280 foreign-born Swedes and 1,390 second-generation Swedish Americans, the result of both migration into the city from surrounding areas as well as population increase. Yet Swedes were a small minority of the city's ethnic population (3.8 percent in 1900, 3.1 percent in 1920). They were far outnumbered by immigrants from the Netherlands, Poland, Germany, and Canada. Most of the Scandinavians lived on the west side of the Grand River near German and Polish immigrant communities and near the furniture factories where they worked. The Swedish American community of Grand Rapids established many voluntary associations, including a Swedish Rifle Club and the Swedish Norden Society, which was first organized as a mutual aid society in 1871. There were several Swedish American publications, including the *Svenska Veckobladet,* a weekly journal published in 1887 by C. A. Wickstrom. In early 1889 it became a monthly journal, the *Skriftens-Tolk.*[29]

Grand Rapids had several Swedish American churches. The Swedish Evangelical Lutheran Church was started in 1871 by Carl Nordberg, a sea captain, who began holding religious services at local Swede John Hempel's home, where Nordberg boarded. A ladies sewing circle was organized to raise money to fund missionary work among the Swedes of the city. For several years, the church relied upon visiting ministers, but in April 1873, sixteen members officially incorporated, purchased land, and began to raise money for a building, completed in 1874.[30]

Efforts to organize a Mission Friends church began in 1875 with a missionary lay preacher from Chicago, Carl Johan Magnuson, who stopped in Grand Rapids. While boarding with the Hempels, Magnuson was surprised to find a small group of Mission Friends in the predominantly orthodox Lutheran community. One of them was John Rose, a furniture maker who had recently moved to the city from Sparta. Rose doubted that there were enough Friends to organize a church, but he was willing to try, and the small group persevered. Their services attracted some curious orthodox Lutherans, but most boycotted the meetings—because Magnuson was a *"bond-präster,"* as orthodox Lutherans called missionary lay preachers—and they harassed the Mission Friends both at work and at prayer. When a meeting at J. P. Nelson's harness shop was organized in 1879, it was interrupted by a mob of Swedes who stood outside hooting and shouting. Through the 1870s, Magnuson encouraged circuit pastors to visit the city, but not much progress was made until a larger group of Friends arrived in 1880 and the Swedish Mission Church, now the Evangelical Covenant Church, was organized. There was also a Swedish Baptist church in the city.[31]

By the end of the nineteenth century, Swedish people living in and migrating to lower Michigan could no longer easily find the employment opportunities and land availability that had drawn so many of them in previous decades. Some moved to the growing cities, but others—especially the newcomers who were still arriving in large numbers—followed the railroads and resource extractive industries into the Upper Peninsula. After the Civil War, this remote region became a major iron and copper producing area in dire need of a large labor force. The Upper Peninsula had attracted some hardy Swedes since the 1860s, and by 1890 it was the primary destination for Swedish immigrants. It would remain so until the 1910s, when the economic focus shifted to the manufacturing industries of the Detroit area.

Swedes in the Upper Peninsula

In the late nineteenth century, the Upper Peninsula attracted large numbers of Swedish immigrants who settled in many communities throughout the region. They felt comfortable in an environment that reminded them of their homeland and offered similar kinds of economic opportunities. At a time of rapid economic growth, Swedish migrants were crucial in the development of the resources of Upper Michigan. The majority worked in mining, lumbering, fishing, processing and shipping, and railroad construction, while others provided food, housing, and other commercial, cultural, and social services. Some sought to farm this cold land, and many combined these activities in diverse economic strategies.

Swedish migration to the Upper Peninsula began during the 1860s and increased rapidly in the 1870s, but it grew exponentially in the 1880s. Rather quickly, twenty-five different predominantly or heavily Swedish communities were settled in the Upper Peninsula. Using the establishment of churches as a guide, one finds that Ishpeming settlers organized the first Swedish Lutheran church in 1870, Calumet and Michigamme in 1877, Bethany Lutheran Church in Escanaba in 1879, Iron Mountain in 1880, Marquette and Republic in 1881, Wallace and Bark River in 1883, Manistique and Menominee in 1885, Ironwood in 1887, Hancock, Gladstone, and Bessemer in 1889, and Crystal Falls and Norway in 1890. Eleven other churches were established in the

"Swedes Porch," boarding house and saloon, Copper Harbor, Michigan, ca. 1903.
Courtesy Superior View.

Upper Peninsula in the next decade. Many of these are still functional congregations, well aware and very proud of their cultural heritage, even though
they have become largely Americanized.[32]

The growth of the mining industry attracted many Swedish immigrants
to the Upper Peninsula, some of them experienced miners from Sweden.
One estimate for 1890 indicates that Swedes constituted about one-third
of the population of Iron County and about one-fifth of the residents of
Menominee and Delta counties. There are four major mining regions in the
Upper Peninsula: the Keweenaw Peninsula in the northwest where copper
predominates; the Marquette Iron Range in the middle of the peninsula; the
Menominee Range in the southwestern area; and the Gogebic Iron Range
in the western corner. Exploitation of the Keweenaw Copper Country and
the Marquette Iron Range began before the Civil War, while iron mining in
the Gogebic Range began in earnest in the 1880s. In 1860, Houghton County
had only one Swedish resident in 1860, but 850 by 1870. Sometimes they arrived in large groups of several hundred, due to recruiting efforts by mining
companies, but if not satisfied with the conditions they encountered, they
moved on.[33]

Mining companies were challenged to attract and to keep the large numbers of workers they needed for their operations, and they did this in various ways. During the Civil War, the demand for copper left the mining companies of the Keweenaw Peninsula desperate for labor, so they collected $90,000 to cover the costs of recruiting workers in Sweden. An agent was sent to Sweden—advertisements in Swedish and American newspapers guaranteed liberal wages—and the workers were not obliged to stay once they paid back the cost of their transportation. Those who did settle down and go to work were considered "good citizens," the "vanguard of the Scandinavian immigration," and "good, industrious, intelligent people." Others were disillusioned by the reality they encountered. One group of Swedes on their way to the Quincy mines near Houghton ran into a countryman who told them that the promises of high wages were false, and that the costs of lodging were high. Although miners were paid $1.50 to $3.00 per day, their earnings were consumed by high lodging costs of $20 to $24 per month. New arrivals in the early fall of 1864 quickly became dissatisfied and refused to work for their designated companies: they "boldly and defiantly resisted all efforts to make them fulfill their written contracts." When the U.S. Army offered an enlistment bounty of $400, about forty of these Swedes volunteered to go to war, and many reportedly fell while fighting on the Tennessee front. Dismissed by some reports as the "baser sort—the scum of cities and discharged soldiers," many veterans returned to become prominent local citizens.[34]

Throughout the country, the managers of many industries tried to decrease job turnover and increase community stability by offering incentives like company housing, stores, and subsidized health care. They provided support for local institutions such as churches and schools, and discouraged or prohibited saloons. This strategy, known as "corporate paternalism," sometimes generated resentment and opposition to the many rules and regulations, but it was generally quite successful. In 1898, Calumet and Hecla Mining Company President Alexander Agassiz told his managers not to make men work on Sunday unless necessary because there were so many Christians. By 1915, when production was slowing down, the mine's manager, James MacNaughton, turned down a request from the Swedish Methodist Episcopal Church for help in replacing their heating plant. He reasoned that it made sense for mining companies to help churches get started, but once they were established, congregations had to take care of themselves "because if we start [helping them] they'll all want some."[35]

Initially, class differences were not hugely significant in towns where so many people worked in the same industry (although ethnic divisions were common), but tensions between populations of stable, family-based, more-or-less permanent citizens and younger, often transient male workers were clearly evident. Saloons, including those run by Swedes, proliferated in mining communities with large numbers of young male workers because they provided a place for social interaction and political discussion as well as relaxation and refreshment. These important functions were often ignored by disapproving observers, thus the historical record usually documents the activities of the 'respectable' folks, who were consistently praised as hard-working, devout, and productive members of their communities. The more transient and 'disrespectable' types were certainly present, and sometimes the community intervened to evict them. For example, in 1882 the [Houghton] *Daily Mining Gazette* told the tale of "Swede Pete" who "had purchased a small house on Seventh . . . and opened an 'all night house' as it were." Although the paper did not give the reason, Swede Pete got the message that she was not welcome in the neighborhood, because a week later, she had "hied herself to a more congenial clime."[36]

Mine owners also had distinct preferences for some groups over others, and they liked Swedish workers because they had a reputation for hard work, stability, and temperance. In 1910, George Erickson, a Swedish miner on the Gogebic Range, wrote home that he was "glad that I am not home but here where I am, for as far as the economy and working conditions are concerned America is far ahead of Sweden for a poor workingman. . . . At the same time you have to be clever, a good worker, and reliable. A man who drinks a lot has no future here. There are so many people that they have demands on a man; but otherwise the Swedes are highly valued as workers, so highly that even if you go and ask for work the boss may ask if you are Swedish, in that case you get work right away."[37]

These prejudices became more evident as migration from southern and eastern Europe increased exponentially after 1890. Many Americans were quite hostile to these "New Immigrants" due to their poverty, lack of education, religious preferences (often Catholic or Jewish), and alleged radical tendencies. By contrast, the "Old Immigrants," like the Scandinavians, were

far more acceptable since they were usually Protestants and highly motivated to assimilate. The immigrants themselves were often quite sensitive
about these issues. For example, when the *Copper Country Evening News*
reported in 1897 that less than 10 percent of the local schoolchildren were
"Americans" (both parents born in the United States), the mother of one of
the 180 local Swedish American pupils "wrote [to the paper] explaining that
she was a German and her husband a Swede, 'therefore little Willie is American.'" The mining communities of the Keweenaw, centered in Houghton
County, were extremely multiethnic, especially after the 1890s when Finns,
Italians, Poles, and other southern and eastern Europeans predominated.
Many of the "Swedetowns" of the area, such as the ones established by
Calumet and Hecla Mining Company and Quincy Mining Company, were
comprised of far fewer Swedes than residents of other nationalities, at least
by the early 1910s.[38]

In the early years, the Scandinavians often organized and lived together,
at least until sufficient numbers allowed them to create their own ethnic associations. Reportedly when the Finns began to arrive in the area after the
Civil War, the Swedes opened their churches to the new arrivals—but differences often arose (especially in churches) and led to separate organizations.
As early as 1867, Quincy had a Scandinavian Evangelical Lutheran Church.
In Calumet, the Lutheran church was organized in 1877 by Swedes, Finns,
and Norwegians. Until 1921, when the church merged with the Dollar Bay
(predominantly Swedish Finns) and Hancock congregations, services were
in Swedish; afterward, they switched to Swedish and English, and finally to
English in 1937. By 1900 in Calumet there were over thirty churches near
the mine, and the Lutherans alone had four churches: German, Swedish,
Norwegian, and French. By this time there were enough Swedes to establish
their own community organizations—including churches, choirs, festivals,
benevolent societies, and newspapers—in the principal towns of Houghton-
Hancock and Calumet. The Swedish Woman's Club was formed in 1902 and
its members cooperated with local Finnish women on achieving progressive
social legislation, including the right to vote, a controversial issue in all these
countries at that time. (Finland gave women full suffrage in 1906; Norway in
1913; and Sweden in 1921).[39]

Workers had their own ideas about what kind of work they wanted to do
and how to do it, and their preferences were subtly expressed in employment

patterns. One young Swedish Finnish woman, Emma Huhtasaari, emigrated in 1903 to join her brother, John, a miner in Hancock. Emma initially worked as a domestic worker, but by early 1907 she had married "a good husband. He is no drinker like some of them here," but she added that her husband, Valter, "is getting tired of digging in the mine the whole time, and emigrants keep arriving in crowds and there are also people without work. Last month ten thousand emigrants landed from the old country." As this letter indicates, Swedes tended to avoid working underground when possible, and many did have the skills necessary to keep them above ground in the mills and machine shops. This was especially true after 1900, when Swedish immigrants were more likely to be skilled workers, and waves of "New" immigrants arrived to take the dangerous and lower paying jobs deep in the earth.[40]

Mine operators actively repressed labor activism and considered Swedish workers to be unlikely participants, but sometimes they were surprised. In Sweden, as in the United States, the trade union movement expanded with the growth of industrialization and with the rising influence of socialism. Large strikes began in Sweden in the 1880s, the Swedish Social Democratic Labor party was established in 1889, the Swedish Federation of Labor was organized in 1898, and an anti-socialistic Swedish Workers Union was founded in 1899.[41] Concurrent with an effort to extend the suffrage, the Swedish labor movement pushed for and achieved a series of new protective labor laws far more advanced than those in the United States at the time. There was a series of strikes and lockouts between 1903 and 1909, escalating into a general strike in 1909 which involved almost 300,000 workers. The strike was lost and union membership declined by half, partly because many of the unhappy participants emigrated. In America, however, one rarely encounters Swedish labor activists in the documentary record, but isolated references make it plain that they were sometimes involved. For example, when a major recession hit the United States in 1873, employers all over the country responded by reducing wages and cutting production, sparking a wave of labor unrest. On the Marquette Range in 1874, miners walked out of the Lake Superior Mine and on to several other major mines in the area, threatening, then attacking workers who refused to join them. The Marquette *Mining Journal* reported that leaders of this strike were Swedes, which very much surprised the president of the Cleveland Iron Mining Company, Samuel L. Mather. After it was all over, he wrote to one of his agents: "I understand the strikers are Swedes and

Norwegians & that the Irish & Cornishmen did not join them.—I am surprised at this for I supposed the former were steady, reliable men, who could be depended on." The strike was crushed when Michigan's governor sent in the state militia and the strike leaders were arrested. The *Mining Journal* reported that the Swedish strikers were soon "leaving in squads, by every train."[42]

In 1911, George Erickson explained why a Swedish miner might consider it prudent to remain on the sidelines during labor conflicts. Describing a mine shutdown in Iron River, on the Gogebic Range where he worked, Erickson noted, "The workers can never win in this case because the employers lose nothing in any event. They have so much ore unsold that they don't care if the mine is closed down for a year or so." He observed, "The workers there were almost all Italians and they have money enough to go back to Italy again, every one of them," but returning home was evidently not an option for him. Erickson did not condemn the formation of the union, however, or the Finns and Italians who headed this effort. In fact, his letters frequently told of his amusing interactions with mining partners of various nationalities. In April, he wrote: "I have an Italian for a partner now, so I am not with the Finns any more. . . . Sometimes we are real good friends and sometimes we fight. He is quite a good worker . . . [but] he doesn't understand a bit of English, so when I say anything he thinks I am scolding him because then he gets mad and starts swearing in Italian." Erickson had his own problems with English: he was able to understand spoken English, but when he tried to speak, it came out "half English and half Swedish." As far as reading the language, it "is like putting Latin in front of the cat, for it is not pronounced anything like it is spelled and there are many words with letters that are never heard when they say the word." By November, both of the men were at least fluent enough in English to allow discussions of current events. Erickson wrote that his partner "said that if Italy would go to war with Sweden they would give the Swedes a real licking, but I tell him that all the Italians would freeze to death long before they got a glimpse of Sweden. I think it is fun to tease him because he gets so mad." In September 1914, just after World War I had begun, Erickson remarked, "It is strange to see so many kinds of people gathered together in a country and still there are no quarrels. Here Germans and Frenchmen work side by side with Russians and Italians, here no one is no better than the other unless one is a better worker than the other. America is a marvelous land, all in all."[43]

Such was the life of a Swedish miner in the Upper Peninsula. Given the dangerous and difficult labor, the corporate paternalism and anti-union sentiments of the owners, and the erratic nature of production, it is not surprising that many of them preferred to work in the auxiliary industries that supported the mines and the local communities—especially fishing, farming, railroad construction, logging, and the production of charcoal for the smelters. Many Swedes worked for wages while they located land for farming and logging, then claimed homesteads, established farms, and sent for their families in Sweden. Sometimes this process could take years, with the men engaging seasonally in these various occupations.

One of these early Swedish settlements in the Upper Peninsula was Skanee, a farming community on Huron Bay in Baraga County, at the south end of the Keweenaw Peninsula. The first settler in the area, Walfrid Been, was born in Helsinborg, Sweden, the youngest of many children of a merchant father. Been went to sea, then eventually settled in Saginaw as the part owner of a Great Lakes schooner. After some business reversals, he decided to move to Lake Superior, settling temporarily in L'Anse in 1858 while he scouted the area and started a fishing business, salting and packing fish to send to Chicago. Impressed by the forest resources, the potential for commercial fishing and shipping, fertile soil, and the possibility of mineral deposits in the Huron Mountains, he decided to settle permanently in 1860. Been married, but his wife died within a year, and in 1864 he went back to Sweden to visit his family, where he remarried. Returning to Michigan, he filed a homestead claim with his in-laws. Other Swedes soon followed, and they officially established the town of Skanee in 1871. Most of the residents were wheat farmers or fishermen, although many moved into lumbering in the 1870s to supply wood for the Calumet and Hecla mines. Other Swedes in the county worked in local slate quarries, charcoal kilns, and railroads. Been prospered as he ran his farm, fished, opened a general store, and operated a sawmill. He lobbied the state legislature to build a road, which was completed in 1874; in the same year Arvon Township was organized, and Been became the first supervisor. When the post office was established in 1876, Been was appointed postmaster, serving until his death in 1907. Been's grandson, Walfrid Been, a mining engineer, was professor and head of the department of Mining Engineering at Michigan Technological University.[44] After 1898, Swedish and Finnish farmers began to settle in nearby Covington following the path of the Duluth, South Shore, and Atlantic Railway. By 1900, there were a total of 438 Swedes in Baraga County, where they were the largest group (26 percent) of the foreign-born population. In both towns Swedes and Norwegians had their own churches. The Swedish Zion Lutheran Church was organized in Skanee in the late 1880s, and the church, built in 1892, still stands. There was also a Swedish Finnish Benevolent Society.[45]

In the middle of the Upper Peninsula, Swedish immigrants settled throughout Marquette County, where the town of Marquette was the area's primary harbor and commercial center. In 1865, three Swedish immigrants arrived in Marquette County—where one Swedish plasterer was already in residence—and others soon followed. By 1870, Marquette County had a total of 1,013 Swedish-born residents (but only sixty-seven Swedes lived in the town of Marquette). These numbers rapidly increased to 2,673 Swedish-born inhabitants in the county in 1880 and 4,303 in 1890. Though the number decreased to 3,190 in 1900; 2,766 in 1920; and 1,469 in 1930, the number of American-born children of Swedish heritage was growing. Larger towns with more diverse economies, like Marquette—an ore processing and shipping center—attracted businessmen and skilled craftsmen. An early biographical survey of Marquette County identified twenty-three notable Swedish locals, including two builders and contractors, one editor, one physician, one mining foreman, one section boss, and seventeen merchants—five of them in the saloon business. The town of Marquette had a sufficient number of Swedes to support several Lutheran, Methodist, and Baptist churches. The Swedish Evangelical Messiah Lutheran Church was organized in Marquette in 1881. The first minister, Rev. Frykman, also served churches of Republic and Michigamme. Faith Lutheran resulted from a merger of Swedish and Finnish churches, although it is now predominantly Finnish.[46]

Within Marquette County, the high demand for mine labor made the town of Ishpeming the primary destination for early Swedish immigrants into the area. First chartered in 1857, Ishpeming has been described as a "mother colony for Swedish settlements and groups in other parts of the country," due to the constant outmigration from that town to other areas.[47] In 1870, Ishpeming was an ethnically mixed but predominantly foreign-born community. Eighteen percent of the population was Swedish; another 30 percent were Irish; 27 percent were English; while only 5 percent were American-born persons. The first large group of Swedes arrived in 1868, but many quickly followed—often men who already had experience in mining. For example, when the copper mines of the Atvidaberg region of Sweden declined, hundreds of miners moved to Ishpeming and Calumet.[48] From Ishpeming, Swedish immigrants moved out to other mine locations in Negaunee, Republic, Champion, Michigamme, Clarksburg, the Copper Country, the Menominee Range (Norway and Iron Mountain), and the Gogebic Range (Bessemer and Ironwood), as well as to the ore docks in Marquette and Escanaba (Delta County). People left when these new mining areas opened up elsewhere in the Upper Peninsula, or because they lost their jobs in the depressions of the 1870s and 1890s. One current resident of Skandia, a small farming and logging community southeast of Marquette, recalled how one of his ancestors decided to leave the Michigame area after he asked a local mine foreman for work and was told "you can have my job—I'm leaving tomorrow."[49]

The first Swedish church in Marquette County, Bethany Lutheran Church, was formed in Ishpeming in 1870 as an explicit attempt to bring civilization to the rough woods and its tough inhabitants. Given the large Swedish population of the town, the church grew and was at one point considered to be the strongest church in the Augustana Lutheran synod, yet it had problems due to the constant migration of the local population, tensions with local skeptics, doctrinal schisms, and the difficulty of getting and keeping ministers. The congregation struggled with pastor problems throughout the century, but the church continued to expand. In 1881, the Norwegian members split off, resulting in two churches, and the Swedes subsequently constructed a school and a new church. By 1920, however, a church anniversary volume lamented the loss of young members to urban migration and older persons to death and illness.[50]

In 1871 the rigid doctrinaire tactics of a visiting minister alienated many of the local Swedish Lutherans. His insistence that those who did not agree with his views "could have no voice in any matter pertaining to the church" drove out these "more liberal Swedes, comprising nine-tenths of the population." It also led to the establishment of a new church, known originally as the Free Lutheran Church, which they insisted would be open to visiting ministers of all denominations as long as it was not needed for Lutheran services, "at least until a regular Lutheran minister could be found to accept the call." This episode very likely explains the origins of the Mission Friends church in Ishpeming, now the United Evangelical Covenant Church.[51]

Proselytizing pastors ran into trouble with the rowdy Swedes, too, as one visiting minister, Aron Lindholm, soon discovered. In 1873, Lindholm reported that he visited mining towns on Sunday afternoons and was dismayed to discover that most of the miners "are the kind who like to spend their Sundays in the taverns. When someone came to preach God's word they would not go to listen but would gather outside to ridicule. God have mercy on these fools who are influenced by their glass of brandy and the gambling dens." Apparently on at least one occasion his preaching was cut short by threats of violence. Lindholm also reported his satisfaction that the Baptists had made little progress among the staunch Lutherans, failing to notice (or refusing to acknowledge) that a Swedish Baptist church had been established and a new church constructed in 1872. In addition, the Swedish Methodist Church (now Grace Methodist) was established in 1873, with Rev. August Waldgren as pastor. In nearby Negaunee there was a Swedish Lutheran Evangelical church, a Swedish Mission church, and a Swedish Baptist church.[52]

Despite the strong temperance sentiments of many Swedes, apparently it was possible to run a saloon and still be considered a respectable citizen. August A. Anderson, an Ishpeming jeweler and saloonkeeper, eventually became sheriff, probably because of his skill in handling bar room conflicts. One day a fight in his bar between Swedish and Irish customers resulted in the Swedish bartender shooting and killing one of the Irish patrons. Anderson rushed out from his office in the back and was able to prevent further violence.[53]

Many Swedish people lived in the towns surrounding the Ishpeming-Negaunee area. Michigamme had a Swedish Lutheran church and a Swedish Methodist Episcopal church, and there were Swedish Lutheran churches in the area around the National Mine, as well as in other nearby communities. Like the town itself, Ishpeming churches often served as a base from which churches in smaller towns were organized. For example, in Republic, local Swedish Baptists were unwilling to attend services in the local Lutheran church, and they were tired of traveling twenty miles to attend services at the Ispheming Baptist Church. They organized in 1883, and a Swedish Methodist church was established in 1885. Ishpeming's Baptist pastor, Rev. A. A. Hammar, began traveling to Republic in 1884, where he was assisted by several local lay preachers. Through baptism and further in-migration, the

Baptist congregation increased and was recognized as a separate church. Unfortunately, the terrible depression of the early 1890s struck the new group very hard. As men began leaving to find work elsewhere, the congregation dwindled, and plans for building a church had to be postponed until 1901. By 1916, the exodus of many of the young people of the community made it harder to obtain the services of even student pastors. Between 1892 and 1938, Republic's population declined by half and became predominately Finnish. By 1937, there were only four members of the Swedish Baptist church left. The Swedish Lutheran church had already closed, while the Swedish Method-ist Episcopal church was still holding two services a month for a handful of members. A similar pattern characterized many of the other small com-munities in the area.[54]

Not surprisingly, many of the earliest voluntary associations in the Upper Peninsula were established in Ishpeming, Negaunee, Marquette, and some of the surrounding communities. As early as 1873 the *Marquette Mining Journal* reported the activities of several different groups: the Scandinavian Church Society hosted a benefit concert and a ball at Anderson's Hall in April; in June, the Scandinavian Home Guards (Swedish army veterans) were "out drilling several evenings of each week." The first such group in the Upper Peninsula was a chapter of the Scandinavian Benevolent and Social Society organized in Ishpeming in 1872. Beginning in the 1870s and expand-ing over the next several decades, other local groups in Ishpeming included the Scandinavian Church Society, Scandinavian Hall, the Swedish Home Society No. 1, the Swedish Lutheran Young People's Hall, the Scandinavian Juniors, the Swedish Red Ribbon Club, the Swedish United Sons of America, the Scandinavian Fraternity of America, and the Swedish Crown Society. Ispheming still has two Vasa chapters, the Monitor Lodge No. 163 for men (established in 1909), and Ishpeming Lodge No. 196 for women (1911). In nearby Negaunee and Marquette there were similar Swedish/Scandinavian halls, lodges, societies, and clubs. In Negaunee, these included Osterbotten Hall, St. George's Hall, and the Scandinavian Aid and Fellowship Society. Ishpeming also had both secular and church Swedish-language publica-tions. Conrad Carlson began editing a weekly newspaper, the *Svenska Posten* (*Swedish Post*), in 1882. After Carlson moved to Bessemer, in Gogebic County, the paper was published briefly under the name *Forposten* (*Outpost*) by Mr. Bertilson. In 1888 it became the *Superior Posten* (*Superior Post*), edited by

Nathanael Mortonson (who was also the organist of the Swedish Lutheran Church and a music teacher), followed by Andrew A. Sandburg and Andrew A. Lind until it ceased publication in 1918.[55]

Given the harsh climate and poor soil of the Upper Peninsula, those who wished to farm often moved further west to Wisconsin, Minnesota, and as far away as Idaho and California. Nevertheless, some Swedish American homesteaders remained in the area, especially as the initial interest in minerals and timber began to shift to farming and other uses of the cut-over areas by the mid-1880s. For example, Swedish Americans, many from Ishpeming, settled in several small farming clusters in what are now Skandia and West Branch townships, located approximately fifteen miles southeast of Marquette. At one time this area had one of the largest concentrations of Swedes in the state of Michigan—when the township was split off from Chocolay Township in 1892, the name "Skandia" (meaning "Little Scandinavia") was chosen because of all the Swedes living there. Many of the men began working in lumbering, mining, or railroad jobs, saved their money, and bought a little land that they could farm in their spare time, usually cultivating root crops (rutabagas and potatoes) or hay, or dairy farming. Most of the farms were settled on marginal land, their choices determined more by proximity to local markets than by productivity, so some of the communities that developed were as transient as the mining and lumbering towns they served.[56]

One of the area's original settlers, Gustaf Hjalmar (Yalmar) Bahrman, moved to the area after serving in the Union Army during the Civil War. He came to Michigan because the federal government was offering land to ex-soldiers in exchange for the scrip that had been issued to soldiers instead of cash. Bahrman built a log cabin and hired a housekeeper, whom he eventually married. His brother, Veking, arrived five years later, walking from the docks in Marquette accompanied by a cow, but Veking later returned to Marquette to live and work as an iron molder. The Bahrman potato and dairy farms still operate in Skandia Township, and many descendents of the other early Swedish settlers still live in the area. Not surprisingly, Skandia Township had several Swedish churches and fraternal societies. Anders Sandberg was a homesteader and lay speaker active in the Skandia Methodist Episcopal Church, established in 1886. Sandberg worked as a toolmaker in Marquette, walking eighteen miles to work on Mondays and back to Skandia on Fridays to spend the weekends with his family, work on his farm, and teach Sunday school. The local Swedish Evangelical Emanuel Lutheran Church started with occasional visits by Marquette's Messiah Lutheran pastor in 1892; in 1902, land for a new building was purchased for a nominal sum from the Cleveland Cliffs Iron Company. A dispute arose over the location of the structure, however, leading to the creation of a new church, Bethany Lutheran, on land donated by Yalmar Bahrman. Unfortunately, during the Depression the membership could not keep up with the mortgage payments, and the building was sold for private use.[57]

The small settlement of Carlshend, which used to be the commercial center of Skandia Township, still exists and retains traces of its Swedish heritage. Eleven mostly Swedish families moved from the areas around Ishpeming and Michigamme in 1884. The first settler, Ole Halvorsen (a Norwegian), used a hollow log as a temporary shelter as he identified and claimed his homestead. The post office was established in 1894, the railroad came through in 1903, and by 1915 an article in the Ispheming journal, *Superior Posten,* described a bustling town with four passenger trains stopping daily. In addition to the depot, there was a church and two stores, including that of the local postmaster, C. (Carl) P. Johnson, who also owned a large farm in the area. (The town's name was originally supposed to be "Carlslund" meaning "Carl's Grove," or "Carl's Land," but a misspelling in the official paperwork inscribed the mistake.) Mrs. Johnson was a midwife and an important community leader. The Evangelical Covenant Church in Carlshend (originally the Swedish Evangelical Mission Church), was organized in 1900 with help and assistance from the Ispheming Mission Church, and is still in existence. Once the sawmills closed and the train stopped running, the community declined, but some descendents of the original settlers remain. In 1976, when all mail service in Skandia was reorganized under a single location and zip code, the people in Carlshend succeeded in retaining the name. In July 1984, a centennial reunion attracted six hundred people from all over the country.[58]

East of Skandia, small Swedish settlements were scattered throughout Alger County, which was separated from Schoolcraft County in 1885. They were closely connected to the regional economy especially after a railroad was built between Marquette and Munising, Alger County's major town. Many of these once-thriving communities have disappeared or exist as shadows of their former selves. The dense forests attracted iron companies

Logging crew, Carlshend, Michigan, ca. 1905. Courtesy Ardy Johnson.

(especially the Cleveland Cliffs Iron Company, which dominated production on the Marquette Range) in need of a constant source of fuel for their
furnaces, so there were many charcoal kilns in this area. These were staffed
by Swedes who had worked at building the railroad, especially those who
had experience as ironmakers in Sweden, and supplied by local logging and
farming settlements. An example of an early Swedish homestead, the Paulson
House, is in Au Train, just west of Munising. The two-story log house, built
in 1882 by Charles Paulson, was restored in 1968 and is now on the National
Register of Historic Places. Another early Au Train homesteader was "Swede
Emma" Neilson, who had been trained as a nurse in Sweden, but for whatever
reason—her neighbors presumed a disappointed love affair—she claimed the
first homestead near Au Train Lake and built her own log cabin. Neilson supported herself by farming, hunting and trapping, and working as a midwife
until shortly before her death in 1916. Neilson was reportedly quite a "colorful
recluse"; she wore men's clothing, readily entered into political discussions,
and used language described as "quite graphic and rife with profanities."[59]

By the late 1880s the town of Rock River was booming; today the township is still there, but the town is gone. One of the Swedish settlers in Rock

River, Charles Johnston, was an energetic entrepreneur. Johnston was in the area by 1876, when his three brothers joined him, and until 1884 he ran logging camps supplying timber to build the railroad. When he received a contract to build part of it, he brought in many Swedes to help. After the railroad was completed, Johnston continued to log timber for the mines and for road and bridge construction. Johnston built a sawmill, and in 1889 he organized the Rock River Brownstone Company to quarry local deposits for building materials. Later he opened a store, established a newspaper, and served as postmaster. Another local Swedish family, the Lindquists, did well for themselves by adapting to the changing needs of the community. When they first arrived, they were unable to speak English, but Gustav was a good blacksmith, and his wife, Mary, a good cook, so they soon found jobs in Rock Kilns. When the kilns shut down, they moved to Rock River, where Mrs. Lindquist ran a boarding house "packing a hundred dinner pails after supper each evening." When the railroad came through to nearby Chatham, they moved to that community, where a cluster of fellow Swedes were already living.[60]

In 1888, four Swedish families moved into Limestone Township, south of Rock River Township. Most of these homesteaders had worked in the iron mines near Marquette, and a few did some preliminary digging in hopes of finding another valuable deposit of the ore. When they did not, some returned home to Sweden, and some sold their land to the lumber companies, but others stayed to work in the lumber camps and on their homesteads. The ethnic character of the town shifted after the twentieth century due to the influx of French, Finnish, and Slovenian immigrants who arrived to work in the lumber camps. The changing composition of the community was probably one reason the Swedish Lutherans decided to transfer their church to the Baptists in the 1930s, although a visiting minister from Marquette continued to conduct weekly Sunday services in members' homes. Apparently there were not a lot of organized churches in this township, probably because there were too few people to sustain them, or perhaps because many railroad and lumber workers were more interested in saloons. The most notorious section of the county was in the south around the town of Shingleton (named for the shingle mill). This town was full of working men of many nationalities and rowdy saloons. Its location at a railroad junction and on a major road allowed Shingleton to become a permanent settlement and to survive until the present, although the small surrounding communities largely disappeared with the lumber.[61]

In the northern section of Alger County along the Lake Superior Coast, Munising and Grand Marais were both major wood processing centers with ethnically diverse populations. After the initial lumber boon in the 1890s, Grand Marais subsequently declined but Munising remains an important lumber and paper milling center. Grand Marais had several ethnic churches, including a Swedish Lutheran Church built in 1900, but it was torn down in 1950 after the Swedish congregation joined the First Lutheran Church, originally a Finnish congregation.[62] In Munising, one colorful local Swede was "Hatless Harry" Siabiaskofski, so named because he shocked the local population by never wearing a hat (he had acquired his unusual last name when he was adopted by a Russian family). Nevertheless, Siabiaskofski was a respected member of the community; he spoke seven languages, and was a skilled photographer, a dentist, a social worker, and a Baptist preacher. His wife, also Swedish, gave massages.[63] In addition to multiple saloons, Munising also had many churches, including Episcopalian, Lutheran, and Baptist congregations. Throughout the county, Finnish and Swedish churches continued to use these languages in their services for many decades.

Economic development throughout the Upper Peninsula in the 1880s and 1890s coincided with large waves of Swedish immigration and attracted many Swedes and Swedish Finns to new communities throughout the region. On Lake Michigan, the major focus in Delta County was near the mouth of the Escanaba River. In 1860, there were only two Swedes in Delta County, but 117 by 1870; 450 in 1880; 1,475 in 1890; and 2,053 in 1900. The towns of Gladstone, Ford River, Bark River, Rapid River, and especially Escanaba became major logging and wood processing centers which attracted Danes, Norwegians, Swedes, and Finns. Stonington and Carney also had significant populations of Swedes, enough to establish their own churches: Carney Methodist Church (now Carney Evangelical Free Church, established in 1885 by Norwegian and Swedish immigrants) and Stonington Bethel Lutheran Church (established in 1904). In Escanaba, Bethany Lutheran Church (organized in 1879), built a very impressive church in 1912, with two towers and much stained glass. As late as 1979, the church was still holding some services in Swedish. The Evangelical Covenant Church, constructed in 1888, celebrated its centennial in 1988, but soon thereafter merged with the Gladstone congregation. There were also Swedish Baptist and Methodist churches in town.[64]

In addition to all the church societies and the Swedish Temperance Society, there were a number of secular groups in Escanaba, including the Swedish and Finnish Benevolent Aid Association No. 9. The building that housed the association, Unity Hall, is the current home of the Veterans of Foreign Wars. The North Star Lodge No. 27, which also had its own hall, brought together prominent Swedish American men in the community. In 1907 a debate on the question, "Can a reform candidate be elected mayor of Escanaba?" was led by two local pastors and a prominent local attorney, Albin W. Norblad. The Swedish newspaper in town was the *Medborgaren (The Citizen)*, published by Louis Johnson. Advertisements in the paper and notices in the city directories indicate that there were a number of Swedish-owned businesses in town. For example, John Peterson worked in the woods and the mills when he first arrived from Sweden to join his sister, then he opened a shoe store which was operated by his sons until it closed in 1966. Johnson's Grocery was similarly established by a Swede who came to the area in 1903; after he lost his left hand in a sawmill accident he went into business for himself. Escanaba was the only Upper Peninsula stop on Prince Bertil of Sweden's 1948 Swedish Pioneer Centennial tour. After his arrival and the obligatory press conference, Prince Bertil managed to sneak in a little fishing before joining the parade and giving a speech. Cultural heritage activities continue to engage the large Swedish American population in this area.[65]

To the west of Escanaba, Menominee County was also a major lumbering region. The first sawmill on Lake Michigan was built on the Marinette (Wisconsin) side of the Menominee River, but Escanaba developed earlier because of its superior harbor facilities. As the cutting continued and new areas opened up along the Menominee River, lumber companies from Escanaba began to build mills. One of Menominee's prominent citizens, Charles G. Janson, moved to the town to join his brother, began work as a blacksmith and a wagon and sleigh maker, and then later became president of American Rule and Block Company, one of Menominee's largest industries. Swedish Lutheran churches were established in both Menominee and Manistique (east of Escanaba) in 1885, indicative of the growth of these lumber processing and shipping centers located on Lake Michigan.[66]

SWEDES IN MICHIGAN

Further west, good timberlands and promising mineral deposits had been identified before the Civil War, but the inaccessibility of the region postponed their development. Timber cruisers working their way up the Menominee and other rivers discovered iron in 1866, which immediately drew the attention of mining, lumber, and railroad companies already established in the Upper Peninsula. The Milwaukee Iron Company, which manufactured railroad equipment, financed the early development of the iron deposits in the area, beginning with the Vulcan discovery (at Quinnesec) in 1873 and the Chapin Mine (at Iron Mountain) in 1878. The rapid economic development of this area, which soon extended further west into the Gogebic Range, quickly led to the organization of three new counties: Iron County in 1885, Gogebic County in 1887, and Dickinson County in 1891. Swedish settlers were more interested in farms and forests than mines, but when the first homesteaders arrived in 1877, they found that most of the good land had already been purchased by speculators in the early 1870s. The first Scandinavians moved into what is now Dickinson County in 1848. Some were attracted by logging in the 1870s, but the vast majority moved into the area in the 1880s. In a familiar pattern, they usually began by working as miners during the summer and farming and logging their own parcels during the winter. Frequently they stopped first in Norway, Michigan, near Quinnesec—a focal point of early Scandinavian settlement where Bethany Lutheran Church was established in 1880 and a Mission Covenant Church in 1883. From Norway, those who were headed for the mines went further west to Iron and Gogebic counties.

Those who preferred logging went north. For example, Foster City was founded 1886 by a group of Swedes who began as loggers. For many years Swedish was the only language spoken in the local church and school. Foster City's most industrious resident was Swan Peterson, who arrived in 1890, went to work in mines, and then shifted to lumbering in 1898. He bought land near Foster City and began farming, but he also built up a large logging business and later opened a store in nearby Hardwood. In 1925, when the timber was exhausted and the Morgan Lumber and Cedar Company moved out, he bought the entire village of Foster City for $30,000, including nine company houses, the superintendent's home, a thirty-two-room hotel, the mills and dam, company barns, stores, and all the other buildings that had previously served a community of two hundred working men and their families. Peterson continued to operate the mills until World War II (and he also started a dairy business), but this energetic entrepreneur was killed in an automobile accident in 1946. The town still exists, although the population has dwindled. The Felch-Metropolitan community was a little west of Foster City. Settled in 1882, it was another lumber boomtown that had a population of approximately six hundred at one time, with both Swedish Baptist and Lutheran churches, but it also declined in the early 1910s.[67]

To the west, Iron Mountain was the largest mining town in Dickinson County. It was home to many Swedes and Swedish Finns who started moving into the area in the late 1880s. Most of them began as miners for the Oliver Iron Mining Company. According to one estimate, about half the workers in Iron Mountain in 1890 were Swedes, although this figure fails to differentiate between the two groups.[68] In 1934, a traveling representative for the *Finska Amerikanaren* newspaper visited every Swedish Finn family in the immediate area of Iron Mountain and identified 120 immigrants with 270 children. The majority came from Åland, but others came from more than twenty-five other Aolandic and Ostrobothnian districts. Iron Mountain had Swedish churches, a newspaper (*Frihet*, which was published between 1898 and 1904), and a Scandinavian hospital. The area also had a profusion of Swedish and Swedish Finnish community organizations. There were four choruses and an orchestra called the Topelius Orkesteri. The sick benefit association, Sons of Finland No. 13, was organized in 1905; when the group joined the Order of Runeberg as Lodge No. 12, it was one of the largest chapters with about 150 members. Efforts to establish a temperance society were not very successful, but a small group started in Quinnesec in 1903 and remained in existence until at least 1917.[69]

Iron County, located west of Dickinson County, was also home to many Swedes and Swedish Finns, especially in the areas around Crystal Falls and Iron River. In fact, Swedes predominated in this area during the 1880s. In Bates Township, a number of Swedish families had settled neighboring farms by 1885, including Charles Olson, the first supervisor of the township. Township records for 1882 indicate that eight of the ten children born that year had Swedish parents. Between 1890 and 1910, about 90 percent of the approximately five hundred residents of the township were either first- or second-generation Swedes. Many were farmers like Andrew Stromberg, who used his training as a carpenter to build an early threshing machine. Another carpenter, Gust Djupe, was instrumental in the foundation of the local Mission Covenant church. An early arrival in Stambaugh, John O. Westerberg, remained in the mining business and was promoted to mining captain for the Iron River Company. Beechwood was another old logging town settled in 1887 that has now almost disappeared, but at one time the community supported both Swedish Lutheran and Mission churches.[70]

As iron mining pushed further west into Gogebic County, Swedes and Swedish Finns followed, clustering in the towns of Bessemer, Ramsay, Wakefield, and Ironwood (the largest town in the area).[71] After iron was discovered and two mines established in 1878 and 1879, the boomtown of Ironwood was laid out in the fall of 1879 and a railroad line was constructed. In the first year, two mines, three boarding houses, two stores, and a restaurant were established to support the large numbers of miners arriving in the area. In 1881, the first church, First Methodist Episcopal Church, was established; in 1882, the Swedish Lutheran Church and the Swedish Mission Church congregations were founded, the latter completed building their first church in 1890. The Swedish Immanuel Baptist congregation organized in 1883 and built a church in 1886. Morning Star Lodge No. 1 of the Swedish

Johan Banér: A North Country Original

Although not well known in Michigan outside of his local community, Johan Gusted Runesköld Banér was recognized nationally by his contemporaries as an important Swedish American poet, journalist, and folklorist. Writing in both English and Swedish, Banér published about 5,000 poems, articles, and other pieces in Swedish American magazines and publications. Despite some claims by his descendents of noble ancestry, from his own account Banér was born in 1851 to a poor Småland family and his youth was characterized by limited educational opportunities and much hard work. At the age of sixteen he fell under the influence of a visiting Lutheran minister, but his interest was in learning, not the church, and when pressured to join the ministry, he ran away and joined the Swedish army instead. His career in the army was not a success, however, and after repeated courts-martial and desertions, he was discharged in 1885.

At that point Banér left Sweden and came to the United States, migrating first to Illinois where he decided that farm work was not to his liking either. Banér then moved on to Duluth where he worked at a series of unskilled labor jobs, but in 1887 he got caught up in a strike which he was accused of inciting. He later explained that he had worked at the mill for just one day when a fight broke out between his partner and the boss. Intervening to prevent violence, he landed on the boss by mistake and the two of them fell off the tram platform and down into the yard. When they regained consciousness, neither was in a mood to fight so they shook hands, but the police had arrived and proceeded to arrest Banér. The newspapers were supportive and the other workers considered him a hero, so they quickly raised his bail, and everyone then retired to a local saloon where the owner refused to charge for the beer. Banér remained in Duluth for about six years, working as an agent for the St. Paul and Duluth Railroad. In 1891 he moved to Ashland, Wisconsin, the location of a significant Swedish American community.

Banér began his literary career in Duluth, and by the 1890s he had established a reputation as a contributor to Swedish American newspapers. In Ashland he was asked to help establish a newspaper, *Frihet*, but it struggled financially, and Banér finally left after his partner published a series of anti-Catholic articles in his absence. By 1893 he had settled in Ironwood, Michigan. He published *Frihet* in Ironwood from 1897 to 1906, but journalism did not support his family, so he ran a store and speculated in real estate. Banér had five children, only two of whom survived to adulthood. One daughter, Skulda, also became a writer, and her memoirs, *Latchstring Out*, fondly recalls her childhood and her unusual parent.*

Banér published under his own name and various pseudonyms; his topics ranged widely from humor to folklore, poetry, and political commentary. He was quite a "free thinker," discoursing on religion, politics, and current affairs, while his poems relied heavily upon Norse and Indian mythology. After 1900 he began to blend the two, convinced that early Norse explorers led by Vidar Viking had made contact with the Great Lakes Indians in the eleventh century. In his youth Banér had read an account of this voyage, indicating that after a long passage up rivers and lakes, the Vikings had found a big island with copper, but he had forgotten this story until an unusual event occurred in 1891. As he recalled:

One day in Ashland, Wisconsin in the year 1891 an Indian dropped into the newspaper to see me. It seemed ridiculous that an Indian wished to visit the editor of a Swedish newspaper. He told me of white ancestors from the East. His description of Vikings was perfect. . . . He spoke many words in a corrupt form of Swedish. He said they had been passed down the centuries by his family as a good luck charm. Other Indians verified his claim. I believe the Vikings taught the Indians how to extract copper from the rocks of Isle Royale. It seems doubtful that savages could have recognized the value of the metal without inspiration from more advanced people. The rune told of peaceful relations with them and the return to Sweden with a supply of copper. Where could Indians learn ancient Swedish words except from Vikings? What other visitors to America wore armor? I remembered the Vidar saga, obtained the notes from my trunk, and found the saga dovetailed exactly with what the Indian had said.[†]

The theory that Viking explorers made contact with the Indians of the Great Lakes remains popular, but most scholars reject the idea for several reasons. First, much of the support for these claims is based on physical evidence such as weapons, inscriptions, and architectural remains, but these include forgeries and material markers attributable to natural forces or to Native workmanship. Second, this hypothesis is biased by the idea (revealed in Banér's statement) that early Indians were too "savage" to mine or work metal, although subsequent archaeological discoveries have since proven that they did so for thousands of years.[‡] The Indian's account convinced Banér and for the rest of his life he read widely, tried to learn about Indian languages, and collected and published Native folklore, highlighting parallels with Norse mythology. As a result, by the 1930s Banér was considered an expert on the subject within Swedish American literary circles, but his reputation did not fare as well in Sweden. Swedish American writers in general felt neglected or rejected as too provincial by the Swedish elite.

Banér was also very interested in politics and freely expressed his opinions in his extensive correspondence. During the Spanish American War, he admonished Theodore Roosevelt bluntly: "You were lucky you gained a victory. The only reason you gained the hill was because the Spanish were poor shots. Otherwise you would have been wiped out. It was a nervy thing to do but mighty bad strategy."[§] He also corresponded with Eugene Debs, the founder of the

American Socialist Party, and with Joseph Hillström (or Joel Hägglund—sources
differ), better known as Joe Hill, a famous organizer for the Industrial Workers
of the World and a labor poet and songwriter. Before Hill was executed in 1914
on a questionable murder charge, Hill wrote that he had enjoyed Banér's poetry:
"I think every Swede in U.S. should be proud of your work." Hill enclosed the
following poem, written in English (as transcribed by Banér):

> Dear Sir:—I did receive your letter
> > Of kindness, love and sympathy.
> They made me feel a whole lot better,
> > Those clever lines you sent to me.
> Of course, I am not feeling sorry:
> > I do not fear the mighty foe!
> Here is my motto: "I should worry—
> > My conscience [sic] is as white as snow."
> You'r [sic] right, Sir: your [sic] a bear at guessing:
> > I did "Explore" both sea and land.
> Still I had ne'er the joy of pressing
> > Your warm and sympathetic hand.—
> Now, this may be a foolish notion,
> > But there is something in your name
> That brings my thoughts far o'er the ocean,
> > To shores where bright Aurora flame.
> Where Thor and Oden reigned in glory,
> > Where Vikings fought on raging sea,
> And where Tegner did write his story
> > Of nameless pride and bravery.
> Their Red blood through my veins is flowing:
> > Our principles are all the same;
> No Vikings bold are Ever going
> > To say that I disgraced their name!

Banér forwarded this poem to Theodore Roosevelt, suggesting that he take
an interest in the case and noting that the Swedish American press thought Hill

not guilty of the crime, but it is unlikely that Roosevelt was very sympathetic.**

As a liberal free thinker, Banér remained wary of organized religion most of his life, but a clerical friend wrote after his death: "He was my friend, and I was his, how peculiar it may seem, . . . but we understood each other well, and as he respected my opinion, so I respected his, because he was an honest man, and I believe in the right of man to decide for himself, what he shall believe."††

That is an appropriate tribute to a very unusual man, because Banér was more than a colorful local character. Although more successful than most, Banér's determination to overcome his early lack of education and rural isolation was not rare among Swedish American immigrants and he deserves more credit for his journalistic and literary achievements.

* J. G. R. Banér, "Duluth in My Days," n. d., Box 1, J. G. R. Banér Collection, Bentley Library, Ann Arbor, Michigan; E. W. Erickson, "John G.R. Banér, Michigan's Viking Poet," *Swedish Pioneer Historical Quarterly* (April 1973): 73–93.
† Interview, *Detroit News*, April 12, 1955. He also self published a booklet on the subject, "Viking Mettles," in 1930.
‡ Jeffrey R. Redmond, *"Viking" Hoaxes in North America* (New York: Carlton, 1979).
§ Quoted in *Detroit News*, Oct. 6, 1929.
** Banér to Theodore Roosevelt, Aug. 21, 1914, and Hill to Banér, Sept. 4, 1914 (as quoted by Erickson), Box 1, J. G. R. Banér Collection, Bentley Library. On Hill, see Gunlög Fur, "The Making of a Legend: Joe Hill and the I. W. W.," *Swedish American Historical Quarterly* 40:3 (July 1989): 101–113; also see Nels Hokanson, "Swedes and the I.W.W.," *The Swedish Pioneer Historical Quarterly* 23:1 (Jan. 1972): 25–35.
†† Leonard Strömberg to Skulda Banér, July 14, 1938, Banér Papers, as cited by Erickson, 92.

Finnish Temperance Association (Svenska-Finska Nykterhetsfröbund av Amerika), organized early in 1898 and had 176 members in 1917.[72]

Ironwood was the home of the very colorful Johan Gusted Runesköld Banér. According to his daughter's fond recollections, her father had been a noble officer in the Swedish army, which might have been true, but as a successful newspaper editor and businessman he was certainly a local notable. His daughter, Skulda Vanadis Banér, continued the family literary tradition. Her remembrances, published in 1944, include many descriptions of Swedish life and customs. Among other things, her account is significant for its perspective on the daily activities of women and children, which do not often appear in more conventional historical sources. For example, she recalled a meeting of the ladies' Sewing Society on the occasion of a member's birthday. As the ladies all arrived with gifts, including a Bible, they drank coffee and chatted about friends and family members. Yet Banér realized that some of the ladies clearly disapproved of one of the guests, a local saloon and boardinghouse keeper they had nicknamed "Johnsonska-pä-Loppan"

("Mrs. Johnson-on-the-Flea"). Brightly dressed, Mrs. Johnson breezed in with a bottle of "tonic," which she advised the other ladies to drink before bed, especially on cold nights: "Take all you like. . . . There's more in the saloon. Eighty per cent alcohol, it is!" Scandalized, one of the other ladies immediately got up "with her Bible in her hands" and suggested a prayer and a hymn. Unfazed, Mrs. Johnson replied that she would love to sing, but the other women replied "standing stiffer," that "the kind of songs we sing are hardly the songs you hear at The Flea, Mrs. Johnson." When the hymn ended, "Mrs. Johnson suggested another, a *slagdäng ä* [apparently a love song] which caused all the other ladies to make different kinds of sounds in their noses." Skulda piped up: "That's a good one . . . Specially that part about—" but she was cut off when the women opened her Bible and everyone got on their knees to pray—perhaps to protect young Skulda from such profane ways.[73]

Skulda Banér's book is full of episodes illustrating tensions within Swedish communities due to class differences and conflicting moral values, but the boundaries were flexible. In another incident, Skulda informed her mother that Grandfather Peter would not be joining them for dinner that evening because she had encountered him as he came out of one saloon and headed into another. From the way her mother's face tightened, Skulda realized that Grandfather Peter was apparently headed to the seamy side of town, "Across-the-River." She recalled, "Respectable girls didn't go there, or they were 'licked' for it, but everyone was aware that the area was full of saloons—and worse." When the ladies did discuss it, "what they talked about was the Women. And then their mouths grew very, very straight." Grandfather Peter disappeared and was gone for several days, but returned in time to officiate at the funeral for a young girl. When he stepped forward to conduct the service, Skulda could hardly believe this was the same man "who took me on his knee and taught me [naughty] songs when my mother or father was not around to hear." Grandfather Peter opened his Bible, but he did not need it because "he knew all the words, anywhere you might open that book." Afterward one of the neighbor ladies said, "As if we need a real pastor in Iron Valley when we have a man like your father who can speak so and bring the tears."[74]

Iron, Gogebic, and Dickinson counties were populated by large numbers of Swedish Finns, although these folks settled in many communities

Johan C. Banér (center) with his friends Otto Elander and Alg. Norén, ca. 1893. Banér, Johan C. collection, box 3, second envelope. Courtesy Bentley Historical Library, University of Michigan.

throughout the Upper Peninsula, attracted by the opportunities for fishing, farming, mining, and lumbering. They worked in the iron mines of Crystal Falls, Amasa, Iron Mountain, Norway, Negaunee, Stambaugh, Ironwood, Bessemer, Ramsay, and Wakefield. The community of Felch-Metropolitan in Dickinson County had a very large Swedish-Finnish population, and at the northern end of the Keweenaw Peninsula, the town of Dollar Bay was principally a Swedish Finn community. Originally focused on lumbering, Dollar Bay's economy later shifted to copper mining and processing. The Finnish Swedish Evangelical Lutheran Church was organized in 1900, but changed its name to First Lutheran Church in 1930 after merging with other nearby congregations. Swedish Finns also established Sion Lutheran Church in 1908, and Bethany Baptist Church in 1923.[75]

Outside the major mineral ranges, many Swedish Finns were employed in the forests and mills of Munising, Manistique, Menominee, Thompson, Baraga, and L'Anse. They fished and logged in Ontonagon in the western Upper Peninsula, and at St. Ignace, Brevort, Cedarville, and the Les Cheneaux Islands in the east, near the Straits of Mackinac. The Swedish Evangelical Lutheran Church Congregation of Cedarville (as it was originally named) was the first church in the area and was used by many congregations. Swedes organized the Zion Lutheran Church in St. Ignace and the Evangelical Lutheran Church in Sault Ste. Marie. In Brevort, Trinity Evangelical Lutheran Church was known for its distinctively Finnish version of the traditional Swedish Midsommar festival (which takes place around June 24). The celebration includes games, programs, and feasting; the centerpiece is a decorated pole, similar to the Maypole in other cultures. The Brevort pole was larger and more ornate than those in Sweden, but it similarly combined Christian and folk symbolism, with streamers, leaves, greenery, and animal figures representing summertime. Midsommar festivals are still celebrated in some Swedish American communities.[76]

Because Swedish Finns spoke Swedish but were culturally affiliated with the Finns, often they were not comfortable with either Swedes or Finns and thus preferred to establish their own community organizations whenever possible. They were active in both the Finnish Suomi and Swedish Augustana Lutheran synods, but tended toward the latter. Their numbers were not large, however. In 1930, the total membership of Metropolitan, Dollar Bay, Ironwood, Bessemer, and Brevort churches (all Swedish Finns) was about eight hundred. At that time there were also five small Swedish Finn Baptist congregations in Michigan, four in the Upper Peninsula (Dollar Bay, Felch, Gladstone, and Negaunee, with the fifth in Roscommon, south of Grayling, in the Lower Peninsula), but their combined membership was only about 225.[77] In the early twentieth century the Swedish Finns became extensively involved in the temperance movement. An early society, the Vasa Stjärna (Star of Vaasa) was organized in Escanaba in 1895 and soon merged with the Good Templars. Similar groups were organized in Gardner in 1897 and Ironwood in 1898, and these then served as bases from which to organize societies in the surrounding communities. When twenty temperance societies merged to form the Finnish National Temperance Brotherhood, twelve of these were in Michigan. By 1902, however, the Swedish Finns decided to form their own national organization. Six hundred delegates representing sixteen temperance societies met in Crystal Falls, Michigan, and established the Svensk-Finska Nykterhets-Förbundet af Amerika (Swedish-Finnish Temperance League of America). Subsequently groups from Dollar Bay, Felch, Escanaba, Quinnesec, Ramsay, Baraga, Jessieville, Hancock, Manistique, Munising, and Newberry became affiliated with this national organization centered in Michigan. Eventually consisting of eighty groups and about 2,600 members, the league held annual meetings in Negaunee in 1903, Ironwood in 1904, and Escanaba in 1907, but it began to decline once Prohibition was achieved in 1918, and especially after it was repealed in 1933. Faced with this problem, Swedish-Finnish Temperance Association and the Swedish-Finnish Benevolent and Aid Association of America decided to merge in 1920, forming the Order of Runeberg (Orden av Runeberg, named after a famous poet). This group, now the International Order of Runeberg, is still in existence largely as a Finnish-Swedish cultural organization, with chapters in the United States, Canada, and Finland.[78]

In conclusion, Swedes and Swedish Finns settled all over Michigan's Upper Peninsula—too many to cover completely in this brief survey. Many of these communities are still in existence, although they have been hit hard by the twentieth-century decline in the resource extractive industries fundamental to the regional economy. This transition has been hard on the people of the Upper Peninsula because they retain deep connections to their communities. Those who find it necessary to leave the area to find work—often migrating to cities such as Detroit, the topic of the next chapter—usually seek to return eventually. Those who remain continue to follow a modern version of a familiar pattern, engaging in wage labor supplemented by farming, logging, and mining. Similar to the members of other ethnic groups, the Swedish American people of the Upper Peninsula remain deeply conscious of their heritage and their history.

Urban Swedes and Modern Times

Although many early Swedish immigrants preferred rural to urban life, cities were home to large ethnic communities and offered job opportunities for men in the skilled crafts industry and in domestic service for women. In the Midwest, Chicago became the most important center of Swedish settlement. With 10 percent of the Swedish American population between the years of 1890 and 1930, it was the second largest Swedish city in the world in 1900. Chicago had 12,930 Swedes in 1880 and 43,432 in 1890; Minneapolis had 3,188 Swedes in 1880 and 19,398 in 1890. In Michigan as in other areas, the urban population increased over time, but the size of ethnic communities depended on various factors. Between 1910 and 1930, Swedish immigration to the United States as a whole decreased, so the total Swedish-born population in Michigan declined, although populations of Swedish-born Americans increased. The decline in resource extractive industries, the growth of urban manufacturing, and major population shifts were other important factors. By 1900, smaller Swedish population centers were losing residents to larger regional centers with diversified economies, such as Grand Rapids or Detroit, which was home to 17 percent of Michigan's Swedish American population by 1930, although Swedes constituted only 1.1 percent of the city's total population.

The Swedish population of Detroit was never very large in comparison to

other ethnic groups, although they represented the predominant Scandinavian group. At first the city did not have a large Swedish American community to welcome newcomers because most new immigrants continued on to
other destinations. A few did settle in the city in the 1840s and 1850s; the first
recorded Swedish resident of the state was Elias Hedstrom, a cabinet maker
who arrived in 1841 and died in 1855. In 1890 there were still only 196 Swedish residents, but after 1900 that situation changed rapidly. There were 601
Swedish-born residents in 1910; 2,659 in 1920 (10 percent of Michigan's Swedish population); and 4,318 in 1930 (17 percent). Detroit's pattern of rapidly
increasing immigration is largely due to the rise of the automobile industry,
which attracted many immigrant workers. In contrast to earlier demographic
trends, Detroit Swedes were disproportionately men: in 1910, 59 percent of
the Detroit Swedish population was male as opposed to 54 percent in the
state as a whole. By the end of the 1930s, there were twice as many Swedish-
born men in the city as there were women. Many of the Swedish men were
mechanics, engineers, designers, inventors, and entrepreneurs who made
important contributions to industry, often forming their own automobile,
machine tool, or other companies. One study of 1,251 members of the Vasa
Order's Fram Lodge No. 267 indicated that 33 percent of the respondents
were machinists or mechanics, and many others gave occupations that
suggested connections to the automobile or related industries. Another
151 men indicated that they worked in the building trades. This sample also
contained 257 women: half of them were housewives and most of the rest
were employed as domestic help, with a few dressmakers, nurses, telephone
operators, or clerical workers.

  A history compiled by the Swedish Engineers Society of Detroit identified
a number of early Swedish entrepreneurs. In 1910, Nels Linar Olson established the Swedish Crucible Steel Company to produce various automotive
products. In 1912, John Markstrum, who specialized in marine and motor
cars, opened his own machine shop company. Otto Amandus Lundell was
president of the Michigan Tool Company, which was established in 1914
and produced a number of machine products, eventually including the first
electric household refrigerator (called the "Isko," Swedish for "Penguin,"
and later known as the "Kelvinator"). George Mattson built Great Lakes
steamships and was considered best marine engine designer in America.
Charles H. Blomstrom, the son of a blacksmith in one of the pioneer Swedish

settlements of Kent County, showed an early talent for engineering. He built a small engine as an adolescent, took a correspondence course, served apprenticeships in Grand Rapids and Chicago, and then returned to Grand Rapids where he built his first automobile. In 1897, Blomstrom moved to Marquette, where he worked as the superintendent of the Lake Shore Engine Works, and where he designed the Superior gas engine and his second automobile in 1900. In 1901, Blomstrom moved to Detroit and established the C. H. Blomstrom Motor Company to build gas engines, boats, and automobiles. In the early 1900s, this company was one of the largest car manufacturers in Detroit, employing hundreds of workers and producing 120 to 160 cars every month, including the "Queen" and the "Blomstrom."[79]

Another important local manufacturer, Carl B. Parsons, organized the Parsons Manufacturing Company in 1913. In Sweden, Parsons had learned to build carriages, and he built the first aluminum auto body in the United States in 1903. In his memoirs, Parsons recalled that he came to Detroit in late 1911 and went to work at Cadillac Motor Company. After about a year, Parsons accepted the offer of a new job as chief body engineer at Studebaker for almost double the salary because he needed the extra money for his own new business. While working at Cadillac, Parsons had invented a concealed door hinge, which he began to produce independently for sale to local car manufacturers, including Buick, Chrysler, and Ford. An important community leader, Parsons served as vice consul for Sweden until he resigned just before his death in 1923. Carl Berglund replaced Parsons as Sweden's representative in the Detroit community. Berglund also had moved from Sweden to Detroit, where he became a tool and machine designer, establishing the Acme Manufacturing Company in 1910. He later diversified into insurance and became the local agent for the Swedish American [steamship] Line in conjunction with his civic duties.[80]

Another significant individual was Carl Edward "Precision" Johansson, who was notable for developing the first set of standardized metric gauge blocks ("Jo blocks") to improve the accuracy of precision-made parts. Johansson first moved from Sweden to Minnesota, then went back to Sweden and worked in a rifle factory before returning to live permanently in the United States. Realizing that efficient mass production would require precise uniform measurements, Johansson formulated the current metric conversion rate (2.54 cm per inch) because the U.S. Congress was dragging its feet on the matter. His standards were adopted by the U.S. government for munitions manufacturing during World War I. Johansson's work also attracted the attention of Henry Ford, who implemented Johansson's blocks in his production process. They developed a strong personal relationship and Johansson joined the Ford operation in 1923.[81]

Also in 1923, the Swedish Engineers Society of Detroit was established by a number of mechanical engineers, architects, tool and die experts, machinists, manufacturers, and designers. Many were inventors and the society has published a long list of their patents and achievements. The charter members included Parsons, Otto Lundell (president, Michigan Tool Company), Thor Olson (president, Continental Tool Works), and Nels Olson (president, Swedish Crucible Steel Company). The group's objective was "to promote knowledge, advancement, and cooperation among the technical men of Scandinavian descent." The organization sponsored technical and educational programs, social events, and receptions for visiting dignitaries, trade commissions, and student and athletic groups.[82]

A Ladies' Auxiliary was formed in 1925, and its first project was to raise money to erect a statue in Stockholm to honor Fredrika Bremer, a Swedish writer and early suffragist. The auxiliary hosted many social events for the Engineers Society, and also engaged in a wide range of philanthropic activities, including assistance to the unemployed during the Depression. In 1940 they organized the Swedish Auxiliary of the American Red Cross. As the Swedish American community in Detroit grew, more social and cultural institutions were established, especially when these groups served as an indication of status and success. Due to the comparatively small Swedish population in early years, many of their social activities involved collaborations with other Scandinavians. For example, Detroit never had an exclusively Swedish newspaper. The Norse Civic Association, established in 1934, published the *Norse Civic News* (in 1975 the name was changed to the *Nordic News*), and in 1936, the *Scandinavian Record* began publication, but its first editor was a Dane.[83]

As always, churches remained extremely important community institutions even as new cultural and civic groups were becoming very popular among upwardly mobile Swedish immigrants. Nevertheless, assimilation and the increasing numbers of native-born Swedish Americans presented challenges. For example, most of the Swedish churches changed to the use of English in the 1930s, hoping to hold the attention of those who were no longer fluent in the language. The first Detroit congregation was Augustana Evangelical Lutheran Church (originally the Swedish Evangelical Lutheran Bethlehem Congregation), founded in 1900 with help from the Grand Rapids District. Unable to secure a permanent pastor, the congregation almost disbanded, but they persisted, built a small church in 1907, and secured the first of a series of regular ministers in 1908. A second church was completed in 1923, and by 1931, it had a membership of about five hundred and still held services in Swedish. During the Depression, the congregation organized a relief society but almost lost their building. They finally paid off the mortgage in 1943, and a new church was completed in 1951. By the 1960s and 1970s, however, the neighborhood had changed and the membership considered relocating, selling, or merging with another church, but the congregation ultimately decided to stay and work within the community.[84]

In 1913, a group of women members of the Augustana Lutheran Church spoke to their minister about the need for Sunday school classes and afternoon services for the convenience of those who lived on the east side of town. These groups were soon organized, as well as both men and women's church societies, and after much discussion, they established a new church, Immanuel Lutheran Church, in 1919. It was a challenge to secure a regular pastor, but the congregation had more than four hundred members in 1939 when the new brick church was completed. Services continued to be held in Swedish until 1938. After World War II, the church recognized the need to expand beyond the small Swedish American community and developed new programs to address the needs of a city greatly altered by suburban outmigration.[85]

Other Detroit Swedish congregations included the Swedish Mission Church (which was established in 1914 and became the Evangelical Covenant Church in 1939), Elim Baptist Church (founded in 1916), Gethsemane Lutheran (established in 1942), and Advent Lutheran Church. Many of these churches shifted to the use of English in their services in the 1930s, but continued to observe Swedish customs, such as the Julotta, the early Christmas morning service. There were other Swedish congregations in nearby areas: Antioch Lutheran Church (Farmington), Faith Covenant Church (formerly Swedish Evangelical Lutheran in Farmington Hills), Dearborn Evangelical Covenant Church, Gethsemane Lutheran (Berkley), and Gloria Dei (Pontiac). The Scandinavian Salvation Army was also active in the area. The

Detroit chapter was established in 1920, and did well initially, building a large temple in 1930, but the repeal of Prohibition and the declining numbers of Swedish speakers led the national organization to close the Swedish Department in 1965. The Detroit lodge of the Swedish-Finnish Temperance Association was organized in 1926.[86]

Ironically, rapid adaptation to American middle-class culture left many Swedes with the sense that they were losing touch with their "Swedishness," but their reactions were ambivalent. One observer has noted that the "genteel tradition" in Sweden had little resonance for people whose own origins were largely rural (from early migrations) or urban working classes (after 1900), so they were selective in their preservation of "traditional" practices. Since many nineteenth-century Swedish immigrants were poor rural people, they were often contemptuous of what they saw as the idleness, elitism, and secularism of Sweden's upper classes, and these sentiments persisted into the twentieth century. Indeed, Swedes sometimes looked down on Swedish Americans as culturally backward and excessively devoted to material self-improvement, while the latter felt that they had already far surpassed their former countrymen by moving to a democratic country that encouraged individual achievement. Later Swedish American immigrants were also far more likely than their predecessors to have been exposed to the influences of Swedish national cultural revivalism. A distinctly Swedish American cultural identity developed in the late nineteenth century especially as memories of actual peasant traditions faded and romanticized versions flourished in both countries. Some scholars have suggested that this was also a generational process: new immigrants remain closely tied to their home countries, while the second generation wants to "Americanize" as soon as possible, so it is the third generation that begins to regret declining ethnic ties and seeks to reestablish these by traveling to the parent country or by establishing ethnic heritage organizations in the United States.[87]

Due to these factors, many Swedish Americans began to organize a variety of new ethnic associations in the late nineteenth and early twentieth centuries. The earliest of these were benevolent societies, but as the Swedish populations of Detroit and smaller Michigan cities increased, many other fraternal, social, and cultural groups were established. For example, there were chapters of the Scandinavian Fraternity of America in Alpena, Dearborn, Battle Creek, Lansing, Grand Rapids, and Cadillac. The Detroit

The Svea Club, Escanaba, Michigan, ca. 1915. Courtesy Delta County Historical Society.

chapter, Du Nord Lodge No. 110, which was established in 1909, combined the earlier practical functions of a benefit society with the new interest in cultural heritage. Its goals were to provide illness, accident, and death benefits; to promote Swedish culture; and "to advance the moral and social status of Swedish people." At first its membership was limited to men, but in 1915 women were admitted. In 1908 two other clubs were organized, the Svea and the Sveas Soner (the former included women members, but the latter was for men only). These were also benevolent societies, offering illness and death benefits, but they quickly expanded to provide entertainment and educational discussions. For example, the members of the Svea club discussed topics such as, "Can a Socialist society be started among Detroit's Swedes?" and "Should women have suffrage?" Although this society struggled to increase its membership, two similar groups were founded by 1914.[88]

One of the most important of the Swedish American organizations, the Vasa Order of America, was established in Connecticut in 1896 when several earlier Swedish fraternal societies located in the New England area decided to form a new organization. At first, some of the participating groups opposed the idea of a national association for fear of losing autonomy, but most hoped it would boost membership. By 1910 the organization had approximately ten thousand members (still mostly in New England), but increasing interest in "Swedish Americanness" combined with the growth of the Swedish American communities in the United States fueled continued expansion. By 1930, the Vasa Order had 72,000 members in 17 districts and 438 local lodges, and chapters were subsequently established in Sweden, Canada, and throughout the United States. The group experienced another surge of growth in the 1960s during a period of expanded ethnic consciousness. It has continued to transform itself into a heritage society as well as a link between Swedish Americans and Sweden with a number of cultural and social programs, including support for education and historical research. In 1996, the group had approximately 24,000 members (including 900 in Canada and 4,500 in Sweden), but it continues to face the challenge of attracting younger members.[89]

In Detroit, the first chapter of the Vasa Order, Fram Lodge No. 267, was established in 1913, but it did not stabilize until 1922, when it began to work cooperatively with the Svea group and the Sons of Sweden. In 1925, it absorbed these groups for a total membership of about three hundred. In 1923 a women's auxiliary was established, and there was also a children's club. They held social events and started raising money to construct a hall, achieving this goal in 1926 (although the building was lost during the Depression). In 1925, members hoping to find a site for recreational activities bought and began to develop a tract of land. Organized separately as the Vasa Country Club, only members of the Fram Lodge were initially eligible, but this requirement was later broadened to include anyone of Swedish birth and descent. Membership increased to seven hundred by 1927 and resulted in the organization of three new lodges in the Detroit area in 1928: Lyckans Stjarna (Lucky Star), We Lodge No. 512 in Ferndale, and Pontiac Lodge No. 510. Other chapters in Lower Michigan included Pontiac, Benton Harbor, Muskegon, and Grand Rapids, but over the years the problem of declining membership and limited resources resulted in the loss or merger of some chapters. For example, the We and Fram lodges of Detroit merged in 1972. Currently there are three lodges in Lower Michigan affiliated with Lake Michigan District No. 8—Flushing (near Flint), Kalamazoo, and St. Joseph. In Upper Michigan, there are five Vasa lodges—Escanaba, Menominee, Marquette, and Ishpeming (where there are still two separate groups, one for women and one for men)—affiliated with the Lake Superior District No.

10. Depending upon their size and resources, local lodges continue to sponsor various activities and affiliated clubs, including sports teams and events, conventions, and ethnic and holiday celebrations.[90]

After Detroit's Fram Lodge lost its building, the Swedish organizations met in a building owned by the Danish Brotherhood, or at the Stockholm Restaurant, which was established by Siggan Sjunnerson in 1939. Sjunnerson had been involved in the Chicago's World Fair in 1933, and then ran a restaurant in that city. Encouraged by friends in Detroit, she opened a local restaurant which soon became a Scandinavian social center until its sale in 1962.[91] The Swedish American Club was another group that met regularly at the restaurant. In 1937, Helmer Akerman established this group with the stated purpose "to further the knowledge of Sweden, its literature, social conditions, institutions and other topics of interest to Americans of Swedish descent and Americans interested in Swedish affairs, to foster social bonds and sympathetic relations between Americans and Swedes and exchange information about the two countries." The organization—whose members included important lawyers, doctors, engineers, businessmen, journalists, and educators—sponsored many cultural events, political lectures, and social events. A branch also was established in Ann Arbor.[92]

The Swedish women of Detroit were very active in church societies, cultural associations, ladies auxiliaries, and other groups. In 1937 the Jenny Lind Club of Detroit was founded, its objective being "to aid in the perpetuation of Swedish culture" through speakers, musical presentations, holiday celebrations, and other events. Its first project was to raise funds for the Jenny Lind room in the American Swedish Historical Museum in Philadelphia, but it soon expanded to engage other philanthropic and heritage activities, including festivals celebrating Valborgsmässoafton (Walpurgis Night, which welcomes the beginning of May), Midsommar (in mid-June), and the St. Lucia holiday in December. Both the Swedish Club of Detroit and the Jenny Lind Club are still in existence.[93]

Like many early immigrants, Swedes were very fond of music. Many personal accounts recall how even poor Swedes sought out opportunities to make and enjoy music, individually or in organized bands, choruses, and orchestras. Much music making occurred in church, but secular musical societies were also popular. There were—and still are—several of these in Detroit, including a Swedish Music Band (as listed in the 1898 city directory), a Ladies Aeiolian Chorus, and a youth group, the Rahlvied Chorus. Early in the 1930s, a Swedish Glee Club was established. During the Depression this popular group, consisting of sixteen singers, gave its first concert at the Swedish Salvation Army building as a benefit for the unemployed. A ladies auxiliary was established in 1938. The club reorganized as the Arpi Swedish Male Chorus after World War II (named for Oskar Arpi, a famous nineteenth-century chorus director in Uppsala, Sweden). This group formed the Arpi Swedish Singing Club in 1952 and built a clubhouse that often provided meeting space for other Swedish groups. For many years, both groups have given concerts; sung for churches, cultural events, and visiting dignitaries; and hosted visiting singing groups as well as toured regionally and nationally. In 1930 the Scandinavian Symphony Orchestra was formed—largely by Danes—and in 1946 a women's auxiliary was formed. For ten years, the Detroit Symphony Orchestra had a Swedish conductor, Sixten Ehrling (the former conductor of the Stockholm Opera House), who performed many works by Scandinavian composers. Ehrling left in 1972 to head the conducting department of the Julliard Academy, but he continued to visit Detroit for guest performances.[94] The Detroit Symphony might have floundered in the 1950s without the fundraising efforts of Signe Bengtsson Karlstrom. A founder of the Jenny Lind Club, and a charter member and member of the board of the Detroit Swedish Council, Karlston was very active in the local Swedish American community. For her efforts, Karlstrom received the Royal Order of Vasa in 1975, the first woman in Michigan to receive this prestigious award.[95]

Education was a high priority among Swedes, thus many Swedish Americans became prominent Michigan educators. Four of the state teaching colleges have had presidents of Swedish descent: Paul Sangren (Western Michigan University), Charles T. Grawn (Central Michigan University), Harold Sponberg (Eastern Michigan University), and John Munson (Eastern Michigan and Northern Michigan universities). In Detroit, Adam Strohm, who immigrated to the United States in 1892, was in charge of the Detroit Public Library system for three decades. Strom died in 1951, but he was honored posthumously when Wayne State University gave his name to its new library building in 1955. Among the Swedish Americans who worked for the Detroit Public School system, perhaps the most prominent was Lilly Lindquist, the supervisor for foreign language instruction for Detroit

Schools. When Wayne State University was founded in 1934, she trained the staff of foreign language teachers. Later she published a textbook, became the first woman president of the American Association of Modern Language Teachers, and won several prestigious awards for her work before her death in 1965. Another notable Swedish educator was Arthur Stenius (the brother of movie producer George Stenius), who made films and other educational audiovisual materials, and later became a professor of education at Wayne State. Other Swedish American Wayne State education professors included Harlan Hagman, George Miller, and Harold Soderquist, while Herbert W. Johnson taught marketing.[96]

In 1963, many of the city's prominent Swedish American citizens formed the Detroit Swedish Council (now the Detroit Swedish Foundation), largely to preserve the Swedish heritage in Michigan and to provide financial support for Swedish cultural and educational exchange programs. The idea of forming a national heritage organization originated after the Pioneer Centennial of 1948, and in 1972 the Detroit Swedish Council was one of the founding members of Swedish Council of America. Currently the council has almost 350 Swedish American affiliates throughout North America. The council supports conferences, exhibits, research, student exchanges, and language, musical, theatrical, and other cultural programs. It publishes a newsletter and has produced several books, including *The Swedish Heritage in America*, by Allan Kastrup, and *Swedish American Landmarks: Where to Go and What to See*, edited by Alan H. Winquist. It also grants awards, including the Glenn T. Seaborg Science Award, given each year to a science student at one of the Swedish American colleges.[97]

Seaborg is an excellent example of the way many twentieth-century Swedish Americans have made major contributions to education and science yet remained actively engaged in the mission of Swedish American cultural revitalization. Born in Ishpeming in 1912, Seaborg moved to California when he was ten years old, but retained close ties to Michigan and his Swedish heritage. Most of his scientific career was based at the University of California, but his wartime research on the Manhattan Project during World War II resulted in the discovery of plutonium, for which Seaborg received the Nobel Prize in chemistry in 1951. This experience must have been a thrill for Seaborg, not only because it is the highest distinction any scientist can receive, but also because it is awarded personally by the King of Sweden. On this trip, Seaborg also participated in a Lucia festival and contest, although these were not customs he had celebrated in his youth. In Sweden, the Nobel prize winners were awakened at 5 A.M. by the Lucia contestants accompanied by photographers, who caught their "startled expressions and rumpled hair" for the newspapers. In the evening, Seaborg enjoyed presenting the winning Lucia with her prize, "especially the requirement that I kiss the Lucia winner many times over for the benefit of the many photographers present."[98] Seaborg served for many years as the chair of the U.S. Atomic Energy Commission and as head of the University of California's Lawrence Berkeley Laboratory, where his team discovered several additional elements, including atomic element 106, which was named "seaborgium" in his honor in 1994. Despite his busy scientific duties, Seaborg often spoke and wrote about his ethnic heritage and the contributions of Swedish Americans to the history of the United States. Until his death in 1999, he remained active in a number of Swedish American groups, including service as chairman of the board of the Swedish American Council.[99]

Many of the Swedish American organizations have worked to re-establish or expand connections with Sweden through travel, cultural exchange, and other programs. The Detroit Swedish Council established the Swedish Language Endowment Fund at the University of Michigan in 1984 and the Carl and Olga Milles Scholarship Fund at Cranbrook Academy of the Arts in 1971. Milles, formerly a professor of sculpture at Royal Academy in Stockholm, made his home at Cranbrook for many years. The Finnish architect, Eliel Saarinen, who was asked to design the facility in 1924 and later became president, asked his good friend Milles to become resident sculptor in 1931. Cranbrook now has the largest collection of Milles sculptures outside Sweden.[100]

In 1988, the Swedish American Chamber of Commerce–Detroit was established "to enhance trade, commerce, and investment between the Detroit region and Sweden."[101] On several occasions, the Swedish organizations of Michigan, particularly in Detroit, have hosted visiting Swedish dignitaries and members of the Swedish royal family. In June 1926, Prince Gustav Adolph (later Gustav VI) and Princess Louise visited Detroit and Cadillac. In 1938, Prince Bertil arrived in the United States as part of the three hundredth anniversary celebration of Swedish settlement in the United States, and in 1948 he returned as head of the Swedish delegation to commemorate the centennial of Swedish settlement in the Midwest. The group stopped in Detroit, where Prince Bertil rode in a parade, gave a speech at the state fairgrounds, attended a number of social functions organized by the local Swedish groups, and even found time for a little golf. His only other Michigan stop was in Escanaba, which organized a similar flurry of celebrations. In 1972, when Princess Christina visited Detroit, she visited Cranbrook and the Arpi Chorus performed as part of a program organized by the Detroit Swedish Council. In April 1976 King Carl XVI Gustaf was the first sitting monarch to visit Detroit, an event commemorated by the publication of a book, *They Made a Difference,* highlighting the contributions of Swedish Americans to Detroit. As briefly reviewed in this chapter, those contributions have been substantial, given the relatively small Swedish population of the city, and reflect an ongoing interest and pride in the Swedish ethnic heritage of the city. In the fall of 1984, the Swedish ambassador visited Detroit to participate in Swedish Heritage Week in Michigan, a series of events, activities, exhibitions, and films organized by local groups.[102]

But what of the present—and the future? In 2004, Jennifer Granholm, then governor of Michigan (also of Swedish descent), established September 12 as Swedish Heritage Day in Michigan, because "Swedish Americans continue to strengthen and enrich this country and Michigan through their culture, pride, industriousness, and commitment to the principles upon which our great nation was founded."[103] In her proclamation, Governor Granholm recognized "over 200,000 citizens of Swedish descent who make important contributions to our economy and society through their commitment to numerous professions, commerce, family and the arts," and acknowledged the important contributions of significant individuals and organizations, including many of those mentioned in this chapter. Thus the Swedish American people of Michigan remain an important and dynamic population group, and there are cultural revitalization groups in several Michigan communities. For example, the Swedish American Heritage Society of Western Michigan, centered in Grand Rapids near one of the earliest Swedish settlement areas, sponsors a variety of events and publishes a regular newsletter.[104]

As important as these activities are in retaining links to the Swedish heritage, the efforts of Swedish Americans to expand business connections with Sweden show considerable promise in helping Michigan deal with the severe economic challenges it currently faces. In 2007, Governor Granholm visited Sweden to investigate the possibility of establishing new business

Michigan Swedish Americans at Midsommar Celebration, Alaska, Michigan, 2010.
Courtesy Swedish American Heritage Society of West Michigan.

partnerships, especially in the area of new energy strategies. In 2008, King Carl XVI Gustaf returned to Michigan to attend the Sweden-Michigan Clean Energy Summit in Dearborn, and he joined Governor Granholm in Flint to help dedicate a project to convert sewage sludge into biogas fuel to power the city's busses. This initiative is a collaborative effort between

Michigan's Centers of Energy Excellence, Swedish Biogas, Kettering University, Linköping University in Sweden, the city of Flint, and other groups. A report on this event by Sweden's Bader TV asked: "Is Michigan the New Sweden?" The report stated that "Michigan is primed to be the nation's home for alternative energy solutions and views Sweden as a role model." This initiative is certainly encouraging, but the contacts were facilitated by longstanding ties between the state and Sweden. If it succeeds, this would not be the first time that the technological skills and entrepreneurial spirit of Swedish people in Michigan have stimulated promising new developments to benefit the state's economy.[105]

Appendix 1

The Significance of Ethnic Swedish Food

ood is necessary to sustain the human body, and different types of foods are also cultural manifestations that help people retain connections to their ethnic heritage, but there is much to be learned from a historical study of the preparation and service of specific dishes in different societies. The ingredients used indicate the resources available in local ecosystems—in the case of Sweden, the heavy use of fish, potatoes (which can be grown in cold climates), berries, and dairy products (every Swedish farm had a cow). It should not be forgotten that many ethnic foods were created by poor people who used everything they could find. When they slaughtered precious livestock, nothing was wasted, resulting in the blood sausages and head cheeses that most modern eaters tend to avoid. Without reliable refrigeration, food had to be preserved by smoking, drying, salting, spicing, or pickling. In addition, the inclusion of new foods reveals patterns of trade and cultural innovation. Potatoes were native to the Americas, and spices from Asia or the Americas, like cinnamon and cardamom, were rare and valuable importations. Codfish, much of it harvested from the Great Banks of North America, fed the masses of Europe for five hundred years. Herring, which is locally available, is ubiquitous in Swedish cuisine. Finally, preparing and serving food is a highly social (and sometimes religious) activity that helps bind people together in a community. Holiday traditions and food allow modern Americans who are aware of their ethnic backgrounds to take pride in the accomplishments of their immigrant ancestors and to maintain aspects of their heritages.

One of the most famous of Swedish (Scandinavian) dishes—one that many people would prefer not to eat—is *lutefisk*. This dish consists of dried fish, usually cod, which is soaked in lye for a week or so to a Jell-O-like consistency, rinsed and soaked again for a couple more weeks to remove the poisonous alkali, then cooked and served with butter or cream sauce. For obvious reasons, the dish itself is not popular nowadays, although recipes can be found online, and some groups still host community *lutefisk* dinners around Christmas time. Yet shared memories of its savory appeal permeate Swedish American humor, stories, and song and help to define Scandinavian American identity.

One widely circulated poem, "Lutefisk Lament" is a parody of "The Night Before Christmas," in which a Swedish American youth watches with growing trepidation as his mother lovingly prepares the dish. As the smell begins to pervade the house, wilting even the roses on the wallpaper, he cannot understand why his uncles seem so eager to eat, but after the dish is served and all the plates are clean, one of the uncles whispers "I'm sure glad that's over for another year." The poem concludes:

> It was then that I learned a great wonderful truth,
> That Swedes and Norwegians from old men to youth,
> Must each pay their dues to have the great joy,
> Of being known as a good Scandahoovian boy.
> And so to tell you all, as you face the great test,
> "Happy Christmas to you, and to you all my best."[1]

Who says that Scandinavians lack a sense of humor?

Christmas celebrations (Julbor) and Midsummer (Midsommar) festivals involved a variety of foods, many of which were also standards in the traditional smorgasbord. Literally meaning "sandwich table," *smörgåsor* are small, open faced sandwiches topped with various combinations of beets, ham, shrimp, eggs, and dill. This light meal evolved into a form of potluck dinner in which dishes are arranged in different categories, then people eat their way through the buffet from appetizers to dessert, washing it all down with plenty of coffee and spirits (if so inclined). The arrangement generally includes:

- First, cold fish: *sill* (herring, usually accompanied by onions, sour cream, and beets), *gravad lax* (salmon cured in sugar, salt, and dill), or smoked salmon. Usually eaten with bread and butter, or with boiled potatoes.

- Next, warm food: *lutefisk,* eel, salmon, sardines, *köttbullar* (meatballs), *korv* (sausages), *koldomar* (meat-stuffed cabbage rolls), *revbenspjäll* (roasted pork ribs), jellied pig's feet, *leverpastey* (liver paté), and *sytla* (head cheese). Served with red cabbage, Janssons Frestelse (baked matchstick potatoes layered with cream, onion, and anchovies), and Dopp I grytan (bread dipped in broth and juices left over after boiling ham). Usually eaten with pickled cucumbers, beets, and salads.

- Follow with desserts and cheeses: *risgrynsgröt* (rice pudding), apple cake, raspberry jam, and other fruits and berries.

- For drinks: coffee, beer, Glögg (sweet mulled wine), and aquavit.

Swedes love to visit over coffee—they drink more coffee than the inhabitants of any other nation—and a variety of sweet breads. These informal gatherings were a big part of Swedish American social life, especially for women.

Mother Liljestrand's Pepparkakor (Gingersnaps) Carolyn Peterson

½ lb. butter	2 tsp. soda
1½ cups sugar	1 T. cinnamon
1 T. molasses	1 tsp. ginger
1 egg	1 tsp. cloves
3¼ cups flour	juice and rind of 1 medium orange

Cream butter and sugar. Add molasses and egg. Sift dry ingredients and add them alternately with orange juice and rind. Refrigerate until well chilled—even overnight.

Roll out about ⅛ inch (not terribly thin) on a floured board and cut with cookie cutters. Bake at 425° until brown, about 7 minutes. Yield about 6 dozen.

Recipe note: A favorite at the holidays!

Recipe from *Swedish Favorites* Cookbook by Swedish American Heritage Society of West Michigan

Another very old Swedish tradition involves eating pancakes on Thursdays:

Swedish Pancakes (Pannkakor) *Ulla Hjelm*

4 eggs	½ tsp. salt
2½ cups milk	1 tsp. sugar
1 cup flour	margarine for frying

Whisk ingredients together. Let stand for ten minutes. Heat round pan to medium heat.

Melt ¼ teaspoon of margarine in pan. Pour in about half a cup of batter, depending on the size of the pan. It is easier to flip the pancake if it is not too large in size. Cook until top is settled, flip over, and cook until golden brown. Fold in half and transfer to serving plate.

Recipe note: Serve with lingonberry preserves or other jam. A common way is to put jam on top of pancake and then roll it up.

Recipe also works well as an oven pancake. Pour batter into greased baking pan. If desired add cubed ham or cooked bacon cut into small pieces. Bake in 375° oven about 40 minutes, or until knife comes out clean.

Recipe from *Swedish Favorites* Cookbook by Swedish American Heritage Society of West Michigan

What Swedish American has not enjoyed a version of his or her grandmother's Swedish meat balls? There are probably as many variations of this basic dish as there are Swedish grandmothers:

Swedish Meatballs (Köttbullar) *Marda (Kapp) Mills*

1 egg	2 slices bread, torn
1 small onion, chopped	milk
1 tsp. salt	1 lb. ground beef (or half lean
¼ tsp. ground allspice	ground pork)

In a blender, blend together the egg, onion, salt, allspice, bread, and enough milk to make a thick mixture. Mix the blended mixture into the meat with your hands. The mixture needs to be stiff to make it possible to form small meatballs. Using a small bowl of cold water, dipping your hands in and out, form the meatballs and place them closely side-by-side in a baking pan. To store them in your freezer before baking, pour ¼–½ cup water over them in the pan, cover with plastic wrap, and then with foil (to prevent the smell of onions in your freezer). On serving day remove the foil, remove and discard the plastic wrap, recover the pan with the foil, and bake in a 350° oven for up to an hour. Gently stir once as they bake. Before serving, drain off the fat and juices.

Recipe from *Swedish Favorites* Cookbook by Swedish American Heritage Society of West Michigan

A simple and refreshing salad that complements heavy meat and cheese dishes:

Swedish Cucumbers (Inlagd gurka) *George Trowbridge*

1 English cucumber, thinly sliced
salt
white pepper
½ cup sugar

½ cup white vinegar
½ cup water
chopped parsley

Sprinkle cucumber slices with salt and pepper. Mix sugar, vinegar, and water and pour over cucumber. Add parsley and stir. Cover and refrigerate for at least two hours before serving.

Recipe note: Use a Swedish cheese plane for perfect slices.

Recipe from *Swedish Favorites* Cookbook by Swedish American Heritage Society of West Michigan

If one is not fortunate enough to have a Swedish grandmother, many versions of these recipes, as well as many others, can be found online.

The St. Lucia Day Tradition

Historians have observed that many national cultural practices and "traditions" are not really very traditional nor very old—perhaps not even native to that particular country. Still they are important and serve various functions. Sometimes they help establish or reinforce the authority of rulers; sometimes they reflect fears that important connections to national history are being lost due to modernization and globalization. In Sweden, where a cultural revival movement developed in the late nineteenth century, a notable example of this process was the institutionalization of the St. Lucia Day festival. While this celebration has roots in pre-Christian winter festivals, the traditional centerpiece of the Swedish Christmas season was the Julotta church service. Nevertheless, the Lucia celebration has become very widespread in Scandinavia, some of the Baltic states, and in Swedish American communities.

The name "Lucia" means "light" (or "the bearer of light") and the saint and her holiday represent this concept in several different ways. In the Catholic religion, Saint Lucy was a young woman living in Syracuse, Sicily (she is the patron saint of that city), who was martyred in the early fourth century. Not much is known about her historically, but there are various legends. In one story, she was engaged to be married, but when she became a Christian and tried to convert (or rejected) her pagan fiancé, he denounced her to the

Roman authorities and thus she met her fate. Some say that her suitor thought her eyes were so lovely that she took them out and gave them to him, but in another version, the Emperor Diocletian pulled them out during torture. Either way, God then gave her an even more brilliant pair. Some accounts say that the candles she wears on her head symbolize the fire that refused to cooperate when she was sentenced to burn, but there is a food connection, too. Supposedly, wearing candles on her head in order to see in the dark, Lucia took provisions to persecuted Roman Christians who were hiding in the catacombs. Interestingly, the Sicilians tell that she brought food during a famine, and a similar legend occurs in Sweden. One winter during a terrible famine, on the longest night of the year, a mysterious ship suddenly appeared on Lake Vänern with a woman (St. Lucy)—dressed in white and radiating light—who helped guide the ship into port and then delivered its cargo of food.

Sweden is very far from Sicily, so how did a Catholic Sicilian saint wind up as the focus of a major holiday in Sweden, now a staunchly Protestant country? No one really knows. In Sweden, the custom is of fairly recent vintage, but it was grafted onto ancient roots. Prior to the Reformation, her saint's day (December 13) would have been important, but significantly it was the date of the winter solstice under the old Julian calendar. Many cultures commemorate this important transitional moment—the shortest day and the longest night—with festivals celebrating the struggle between the forces of light and dark. In Sweden, Yule (Jo'l) was originally such a winter solstice celebration, with plenty of feasting, drinking, and celebration, but also a certain degree of fear and apprehension. In pre-Christian Sweden, December 13 was Lussinatta or Lussi Night, when Lussi, an evil female spirit, began nightriding with her followers continuing until Yule. At this time, everyone (especially naughty children) had to be on guard against various demons, spirits, and trolls who might carry them off. Some scholars point to the similarities in the names (Lucia and Lussi) and the common date as sufficient to explain the transplantation of the saint's story to Sweden. Others connect the Lucia symbolism with Freya, the beautiful Norse goddess of love (also battle, death, and wealth), who rode around in a chariot pulled by cats. Freya was the sister of the god Frey, to whom sacrifices were made at Yule. Thus pagan winter celebrations became Christianized, although both the Catholic and Protestant churches generally condemned traditional practices as heathen superstitions or diabolical manifestations.

Some have noted that the figure of Lucy is similar to the German Protestant practice of the Christkindchen (Christ Child), in which a young girl or
girls dress as Christ children, wear crowns of lights, and pass out Christmas
presents. In Sweden, this custom (called Kinken Jes) began to appear in elite
families in the 1700s. Young boys also participate in events throughout the
Christmas season. They might be dressed as angels, gingerbread men, or
as Tomtenissar. Also a holdover from pagan times, the *tomte* was a house
elf or imp. Because he could be easily offended and do mischief, a bowl of
porridge was often left for him on Christmas Eve. In the mid-1800s, these traditional figures became identified as Christmas elves (*jultomte*) who brought
Christmas presents. *Stjärngossar* (star boys) carry star-topped scepters and
are dressed in white robes with cone-shaped hats made of silver paper or
decorated with stars. The boys usually join processions and sing carols, often
about Saint Stephen, the first Christian martyr. The star boys singing proces-
sion comes from a Catholic liturgical drama from the 1500s representing the
journey of the three kings. Because of its Catholic associations, the practice
was discouraged in Protestant Sweden, but the star boys still play a role in the
St. Lucia Day celebrations. According to traditional wisdom, St. Lucia's Day
(Luciadagen) is the beginning of the Christmas season, so by that date all the
farm and house work, cleaning, and Christmas decorating should be completed. Farmers slaughter the Christmas pigs, while housewives start preparing the *lutfisken* so it will be ready by Christmas Day. Finishing so many
chores often meant working well into the night, so sometimes young people
(girls dressed in white, star boys, and *tomterna* children), would go around
bringing food. Thus a long night of work might easily evolve into a party,
especially among the youth. After a strenuous (and potentially dangerous)
Lussi night, animals and people needed a lot of food, so the next morning
was the occasion for a hearty breakfast, perhaps served to the adults in bed.

Incorporating these earlier traditions, the holiday as it is currently celebrated developed in the area around Lake Vänern in the late 1700s, largely
as a private affair within elite families. Early in the morning, one daughter
(the oldest, youngest, or prettiest) gets up very early (usually between one
and four in the morning), and serves the family coffee and cat-shaped saf-
fron buns (Lussenkatter, or "Lucy Cats"). She dresses in a white robe and a
red sash, with a wreath of lingonberry leaves and seven white lit candles on
her head. She might be accompanied by the other girls in the family, or the

boys dressed as *stjärngossar*. Originally the occasion was observed only in upper-class families, but early twentieth-century urbanization and cultural revivalist movements made it a quite popular and often public celebration which spread beyond Sweden into other parts of Scandinavia and the Baltic. Although not an official Swedish holiday, St. Lucia's Day is celebrated in schools, offices, and public festivals. Many communities choose their own Lucy queens and hold parades accompanied by handmaidens, star boys, and Jultomten. In modern times, electric lights have replaced the candles in the headdress, and Lucias can be boys as well as girls (although boys generally prefer their traditional supporting roles).[1] For many reasons, the St. Lucia celebration was not commonly practiced by nineteenth-century Swedish immigrants in the United States. It was an elite urban custom that would have been unfamiliar to poor rural folk like many of the early immigrants, who often were strongly religious. They considered old ways to be pagan superstitions and focused their celebration on the annual Julotta church service. It was only in the twentieth century that urbanization and cultural revivalism made the St. Lucia Day celebration widely popular among Swedish Americans.[2]

The memoirs of Skulda Banér, raised in Ironwood, Michigan, confirm this assessment. She recalled one St. Lucia Day when her colorful and always iconoclastic father, Johan Banér, reversed the custom by greeting her with breakfast in bed, resplendent in "a gold-paper crown on his head with seven candles in it." When Skulda asked him if the other kids had St. Lucia Day he replied probably not: "They can't know about Lucia and her Day unless their fathers or mothers told them. And everybody doesn't know." He explained that, "Their people over in Sweden were *bönder*, maybe, and they had to work very hard, just to live. They had no time to learn about the Lucias or their Days." Skulda's free-thinking father could joke around with a secular occasion, but her mother insisted upon going to church on Christmas. Although Skulda tried to "pretend it is Julotta," she missed the long snowy sleighride and the "very special feeling inside that belonged with no other hours in the year," and she was disappointed that all she had "was the packing-box church." During a fairly standard church service, Skulda's thoughts turned to the packages waiting at home under the tree, and the feast: "*Lutfish*, the jellied veal *sylta*, *the red glos* of the lingonberries, and the sausage and meats simmered in the big iron kettle we would *doppa* our bread into because that was the way you did at Christmas." She was cheered by the thought of the Julgubbe, "who would really be my father in false face with whiskers," but she missed her grandmother far away in Sweden, and felt sad, thinking that Christmas was both a wonderful celebration and yet a time of nostalgia and homesickness.[3] Thus Swedish American Christmas celebrations were bittersweet occasions, a time for reaffirming connections to the home country through traditional practices and for inventing new ones appropriate to life in the United States.

Appendix 3
Swedish Ethnic Associations

- Detroit Swedish Foundation, WEB *http://www.detroitswedishfoundation.com*
- Swedish Club of Metropolitan Detroit, 22398 Ruth Street, Farmington Hills, MI 48336-4249; WEB *http://swedishclub.net*. Organizations in the Club include The Arpi Swedish Male Chorus, Metropolitan Club, Norwegian Men's Club, Scandia Women's Chorus of Michigan, Senior Danes, Sons of Norway, Swedish Club of Metropolitan Detroit, and the Swedish Club Women's Organization.
- Swedish-American Chamber of Commerce–Detroit, Inc., 4750 S. State Road, #312, Ann Arbor, MI 48108; TEL (734) 276-7250; E-MAIL *sacc-detroit@prodigy.net*; WEB *http://www.sacc-detroit.org*
- Swedish American Heritage Society of Western Michigan, 29 Pearl Street NW #127, Grand Rapids, MI 49503; TEL (616) 458-0420; E-MAIL *info@sahswm.org*; WEB *http://sahswm.org*
- Swedish Council of America, 2600 Park Avenue, Minneapolis, MN 55407; TEL (800) 981-4SCA or (612) 871-0593; E-MAIL s*wedcoun@swedishcouncil.org*; WEB *http://www.swedishcouncil.org*
- Vasa Order, WEB *http://www.vasaorder.net*

Notes

1. Amandus Johnson, "Colonists," in *Swedes in America, 1638–1938*, ed. Adolph B. Benson and Naboth Hedin (New York: Haskell House, 1969), 5–34.

2. Ulf Beijbom, "Swedes," in *Harvard Encyclopedia of American Ethnic Groups*, ed. Stephan Thernstrom, Ann Orlov, and Oscar Handlin (Cambridge: Harvard University Press, 1980), 971–981; Florence E. Janson, *The Background of Swedish Immigration* (Chicago: University of Illinois Press, 1931); Allan Kastrup, *The Swedish Heritage in America* (St. Paul: North Central, 1975); Christian T. Feddersen, *Scandinavians in Michigan* (Hancock, Michigan: The Book Concern, 1968).

3. Janson, *The Background of Swedish Immigration*, 117–221.

4. Ibid., 222–316.

5. Jeffrey W. Hancks, *Scandinavians in Michigan* (East Lansing: Michigan State University Press, 2006), 24–26.

6. J. S. Olson to his brother Alfred, 16 June 1883, in *Letters from the Promised Land: Swedes in America, 1840–1914*, ed. H. Arnold Barton (Minneapolis: University of Minnesota Press, 1975), 191.

7. Janson, *The Background of Swedish Immigration*, 355–399; Beijbom, "Swedes," 971–973.

8. H. Arnold Barton, "Old Swedish Traditions," *Swedish American Historical Quarterly* 33:4 (Oct. 1982): 236–240.

9. Henry Hanson, "The Vasa Order of America: Its Role in the Swedish American

Community: 1896-1996," *Swedish American Historical Quarterly* 47 (1996): 236-244.

10. Beijbom, "Swedes," 979-980.

11. Barton, "Old Swedish Traditions," 238.

12. Ulf Jonas Björk, "The Swedish American Press as an Immigrant Institution," *Swedish American Historical Quarterly* 51:4 (Oct. 2000): 269-282; Anna Williams, "Journalism and Ethnicity in Swedish America," *Swedish American Historical Quarterly* 43 (1992): 146-155.

13. Edward Burton, "The Swedish American Newspapers in the Sixties and Seventies," *Swedish American Historical Quarterly* (Oct. 2006): 205-217.

14. Richard Hathaway, ed., *Ethnic Newspapers and Periodicals in Michigan: A Checklist* (Ann Arbor: Michigan Archival Association, 1978), 92-98, 105.

15. Björk, "The Swedish American Press," 270-279; Williams, "Journalism and Ethnicity in Swedish America," 146-147.

16. Historical Census Browser (University of Virginia, Geospatial and Statistical Data Center, 2004), available at http://fisher.lib.virginia.edu/collections/stats/histcensus/index.html. All population figures in this book are derived from the *United States Census of Population and Housing*, as accessed through this web source.

17. C. E. Hoffsten, "Swedish American History in Lower Michigan," in *The Swedish Element in America: A History of Swedish American Achievements from 1638 to the Present Day*, 2nd ed., ed. Axel W. Hultén (Chicago: Swedish American Biographical Society, 1934), 27-50; Grace G. Albinson, "An Early Swedish Settlement in Michigan," in *American Swedish Historical Foundation Year Book 1947*, part 1 (Lancaster, Pennsylvania: Lancaster Press, 1947), 49-54; Hancks, *Scandinavians in Michigan*, 24-26; George P. Graff, *The People of Michigan* (Lansing: Michigan Department of Education, 1974), 58-62.

18. *Grand Rapids Herald*, 5 May 1928; Nils William Olsson, "The Swedish Settlement of Tustin, MI," *The Swedish Pioneer* 12:3 (July 1962): 109-117; Chapman Brothers, *Portrait and Biographical Album of Osceola Co.* (Chicago: Chapman Brothers, 1884), 192, 363-364, available from the University of Michigan Digital Library Text Collections, http://quod.lib.umich.edu/cgi/t/text/.

19. Godfrey Anderson, "Christmas in the Country and the Yulefest at Axel Carlsons," 1966, MS Collection #023, Box 1.6, and "Christmas as the Old-Time Swedes Observed It," MS Collection #023, Box 1.7, Godfrey Anderson Manuscript Collection, Grand Rapids Public Library, Grand Rapids, Michigan. Quote is from

Anderson, "Christmas in the Country," 3.

20. Anderson, "Christmas in the Country," 2–12.

21. Ibid.; Anderson, "Christmas as the Old-Time Swedes Observed It," 1–9.

22. Hoffsten, "Swedish American History in Lower Michigan," 27–38; *Grand Rapids Herald*, 4 Aug. 1913; Alan H. Winquist, *Swedish American Landmarks* (Minneapolis: Swedish Council of America, 1995), 103–111.

23. Hancks, *Scandinavians in Michigan*, 33–34.

24. Velma F. Matson, "White Cloud's Swedentown," Newaygo County Historical Society Collection, White Cloud, Michigan, n.d.

25. Hoffsten, "Swedish American History in Lower Michigan," 38–39; Berrien County Historical Association, "Greetings from St. Joseph," Berrien County Historical Association, Berrien Springs, Michigan, 2008.

26. Hoffsten, "Swedish American History in Lower Michigan," 35–37; *History of Muskegon County, Michigan* (Chicago: H. R. Page , 1882), 129; James L. Smith, *An Account of Muskegon County* (Dayton, Ohio: National Historical Association, 1925). Last two sources available from the University of Michigan Digital Library Text Collections, http://quod.lib.umich.edu/cgi/t/text/.

27. Ferdinand Nelson, "Reminiscences," (vol. 1), 2–11, (vol. 2), 89–94, n.d., Ferdinand Nelson Papers, Bentley Historical Library, Ann Arbor, Michigan.

28. Nelson, "Reminiscences," (vol. 2), 149–150, (vol. 3), 1–55.

29. Hoffsten, "Swedish American History in Lower Michigan," 32–35; Linda Samuelson, *Heart and Soul: The Story of Grand Rapids Neighborhoods* (Grand Rapids: William B. Eerdmans, 2003), 88; *Grand Rapids [Evening] Press*, 4 Sept. 1899, 11 March 1902, 24 March 1903, 27 July 1923; *Grand Rapids Herald*, 13 Jan. 1913.

30. *Grand Rapids Daily Eagle,* 9 Sept. 1878, *Grand Rapids [Evening] Press*, 14 April 1963; Godfrey Anderson, "Early Days of the Swedish Mission Movement in Grand Rapids," n.d., MS #023, Box 1.8, Anderson Collection.

31. Anderson, "Early Days of the Swedish Mission Movement," 3–15; Mission Covenant Church, "This Is the Lord's Doings, 1880–1955," *Jubilee Anniversary Book* (1955), Box 5.3, Collection #262, Grand Rapids Public Library.

32. *Ispheming Iron Ore,* 4 June 1938. Other churches were later established in Carney, Dagget, Skandia, Metropolitan, Perkins, Ford River, Newberry, Cedarville, Grand Marais, Dollar Bay, and Sault Ste. Marie.

33. The *Portage Lake Mining Gazette* reported that two hundred Swedes had landed at Houghton on June 21, 1872; the *Marquette Mining Journal* reported on May 11, 1872 that nine hundred were on their way to the Marquette Range.

34. John Harris Forster, "War Times in the Copper Mines," *Michigan Pioneer and Historical Collections* (1891), 380–381.

35. Larry Lankton, *Cradle to Grave: Life, Work, and Death in the Lake Superior Copper Mines* (Cambridge: Oxford University Press, 1991), 211.

36. Arthur W. Thurner, *Calumet Copper and People: History of a Michigan Mining Community, 1864–1970* (Chicago: privately published, 1974), 60.

37. George Erickson to Linus Paulin, 26 Dec. 1910, in *Letters from the Promised Land*, 270.

38. Thurner, *Calumet Copper and People*, 25; Arthur W. Thurner, *Strangers and Sojourners: A History of Michigan's Keweenaw Peninsula* (Detroit: Wayne State University Press, 1994), 133; Christina Leskinen, "Our Adventure of Witness and Work," 1952, Michigan Technological University Archives, Houghton, Michigan.

39. Thurner, *Strangers and Sojourners*, 133; Leskinen, "Our Adventure of Witness and Work."

40. Lankton, *Cradle to Grave*, 211–213; Emma Huhtasaari to her brother Peter, 12 Dec. 1896, in *Letters from the Promised Land*, 237.

41. Janson, *The Background of Swedish Immigration*, 440–489.

42. Terry S. Reynolds, "Swedes and the Strike of 1874" (Voices in Stone Conference, 18 Oct. 2008, Marquette, Michigan). Reynolds cites the *Mining Journal*, 1 Aug. 1874. Samuel L. Mather to Jay C. Morse, 25 July 1874, Cleveland Cliffs Papers, MS 86-100, Item 1776, Northern Michigan University Archives, courtesy of Professor Reynolds.

43. George Erickson to Linus Paulin, 20 Feb. 1910, 2 April, 20 Aug., 4 Nov. 1911, Sept. 1914, in *Letters from the Promised Land*, 268–276.

44. Marvin C. Hanson, "Skanee: Its Early Days," Marquette History Museum, Marquette, Michigan; Russell M. Magnaghi, "Scandinavians in Baraga County," Marquette History Museum, Marquette, Michigan; Anders Myhrman, "Swedish Finns and Iron Mountain," trans. Syrene Forsman, *Swedish Finn Historical Society Quarterly* (Summer 2005): 68-69.

45. Winquist, *Swedish American Landmarks*, 103–111.

46. For Swedish Americans in Marquette County, see the *Marquette Mining Journal*, 22–24 Jan. 1931 (reports of presentations to the Marquette County Historical Society by O. H. Bostrom, pastor of Messiah Lutheran Church), 13 May 1948, and *Escanaba Daily Press*, 23 March 1941. See also Arnold R. Alanen, "Ethnic and Immigrant Groups in Marquette County, Michigan" in *Historical Resources of the Iron Range of Marquette County*, ed. William H. Mulligan Jr. (1991), available at

the Marquette County Historical Society.

47. Kastrup, *The Swedish Heritage in America*, 207.

48. In 1992, a party of Ishpeming residents on a trip to Sweden were surprised but pleased to rediscover and renew this connection, resulting in a reciprocal visit from an Alvidaberg dance group. Interview with Paul Blomgren, 12 March 2004, Marquette, Michigan; *Marquette Mining Journal*, 2 May 1992.

49. Ardy Johnson, in discussion with the author, October 2008.

50. *Marquette Mining Journal*, 22–24 Jan. 1931; Bethany Lutheran Church, *Jubilee Album 1920*, trans. Ruth Stolen, Gerda Sands, and Helen Bennett, 9.

51. *Marquette Mining Journal*, 25 Nov., 2, 12, 30 Dec. 1871.

52. *Marquette Mining Journal*, 7 Sept. 1872, 22–24 Jan. 1931; Bethany Lutheran Church, *Jubilee Album 1920*, 9.

53. Marquette Mining Journal, 23 Jan. 1931.

54. E. O. Ericson, "The Elim Swedish Baptist Church of Republic, Michigan," unpublished manuscript, June 1938, courtesy of Gregg Wixtrom.

55. *Marquette Mining Journal*, 26 April, 14, 21 June 1873, 22 Jan. 1931; *Escanaba Daily Press*, 23 March 1941. Additional Information on Swedish organizations was provided courtesy of Russell Magnaghi, Department of History, Northern Michigan University.

56. Henry S. Heimonen, "Agricultural Trends in the Upper Peninsula," *Michigan History* 41 (March 1957): 45–46.

57. Paula A. Wilson, "From Yalmar: Its History and Its Community, 1867–1947," 1977, manuscript, Marquette County History Museum, Marquette, Michigan; Carol Bahrman Christensen, "The Bahrman Family: First Settlers in Skandia," in *Skandia Township Centennial*, ed. Judy M. Johnson (Ann Arbor: Braun-Brumfield, 1992), 207–213; Paula A. Wilson, "Yalmer," in *Skandia Township Centennial*, 232–236; "Emanuel Lutheran Church," in *Skandia Township Centennial*, 250–263; "Skandia Methodist Church," in *Skandia Township Centennial*, 238–249. These centennial volumes are wonderful resources, although it is not always clear where the source material came from or where it went—presumably most of it remains with individual families.

58. "Carlshend," in *Skandia Township Centennial*, 115–159; C. Fred Rydholm, *Superior Heartland: A Backwoods History*, vol. 2 (Ann Arbor: Braun-Brumfield, 1989), 1018–1023; *Marquette Mining Journal*, 7 July 1984; Ardy Johnson, "Covenant Church, Carlshend," in *Skandia Township Centennial*, 264–266. I was fortunate to interview Mr. Ardy Johnson, a local historian and direct descendent of C. P.

Johnson, and I am grateful to him for his conversations with me on the history of Carlshend.

59. Charles A. Symon, ed., *Alger County: A Centennial History, 1885–1985* (Munising, Michigan: Bayshore Press, 1986), 74–75.

60. Ibid., 49–51.

61. Ibid., 41.

62. Jim Carter, letter to the author, 22 Oct. 2008.

63. Symon, *Alger County*, 183.

64. *Escanaba Daily Press*, 23 March 1941; *Delta Reporter*, 17 June 1954; *Upper Peninsula Sunday Times*, 15 April 1979.

65. *Delta Reporter*, 9 March 1928; *Escanaba Daily Press*, 15 June 1948, 14 April 2006; Jean Peterson Brayak, "The Story of John Peterson," in *An Ethnic History of Delta County*, ed. Elmer A. Bessonen (Iron Mountain, Michigan: Mid-Peninsula Library Cooperative, 1978), 14–16.

66. Kastrup, *The Swedish Heritage in America*, 440.

67. Roy L. Dodge, *Michigan Ghost Towns of the Upper Peninsula* (Las Vegas: Glendon Publishing, 1973), 103–107, 110–111.

68. Graff, *The People of Michigan*, 59.

69. Armas K. E. Holmio, *History of the Finns in Michigan*, trans. Ellen M. Ryynanen, (Detroit: Wayne State University Press, 2001), 405–412; Anders Myhrman, "The Finland-Swedes in America," *Swedish American Historical Quarterly* 31:1 (Jan. 1980): 16–33; Myhrman, "Swedish Finns and Iron Mountain," 68–69; Anders Myhrman, *Finlandssvenskar I Amerika: The Finland Swedes in America* (Helsingfors, Finland: Svenska Litteratursallskapet i Finland, 1973).

70. Jack Hill, *A History of Iron County, Michigan* (Norway, Michigan: The Norway Current, 1976), 116, 127–132, 147; Dodge, *Michigan Ghost Towns*, 153–155.

71. Graff, *The People of Michigan*, 33.

72. Syrene Forsman, "Swedish Finns and Early Ironwood, Michigan" *Swedish Finn Historical Society Quarterly* (Spring 2005): 38, 58.

73. Skulda V. Banér, *Latchstring Out* (New York: Houghton Mifflin, 1944), 20–26.

74. Ibid., 50–66.

75. Clarence J. Monette, *Dollar Bay, Michigan* (Lake Linden, Michigan: C. J. Monette, ca. 2000), 30–31, 37–38, 59; Holmio, *History of the Finns in Michigan*, 407–408; Myhrman, "The Finland-Swedes in America," 21, 24, 29.

76. J. Philemon Anderson, "A History of Brevort," ca. 1961, in the John Markstrum Collection, Bentley Library, Ann Arbor, Michigan; *St. Ignace News*, 1 July 1899.

77. Holmio, *History of the Finns in Michigan*, 405-412.

78. Ibid., 408-411. For the Order of Runeberg, see their webpage at http://www. orderofruneberg.org/aboutus/history.html.

79. John Markstrum, "Vikings Abroad," n.d., Swedish Engineering Society Collection, Bentley Library, Ann Arbor, Michigan; Kastrup, *The Swedish Heritage in America*, 432-433.

80. Carl B. Parson, "Reminiscences," n.d., Carl B. Parsons Collection, Bentley Library, Ann Arbor, Michigan; Kastrup, *The Swedish Heritage in America*, 434.

81. Kastrup, *The Swedish Heritage in America*, 435-436.

82. Feddersen, *Scandinavians in Michigan*, 215.

83. Ibid., 214-227; Marion Edman, "Organizations," in *They Made a Difference: Highlights of the Swedish Influence on Detroit and Michigan*, ed. Detroit Swedish Council (Detroit: Detroit Swedish Council, 1976), 41.

84. Feddersen, *Scandinavians in Michigan*, 198-201.

85. Ibid., 204-207.

86. Marion Edman, "The Swedish Churches of Detroit," in *They Made a Difference*, 15-25; Clarence H. Johnson, "Origins, Population, Locations, Occupations and Activities of the Swedes in Detroit," MA thesis, Wayne State University, 1940, 66-67; Edward O. Nelson, "Recollections of the Salvation Army's Scandinavian Corps," *Swedish American Historical Quarterly* 29:4 (Oct. 1978): 257-276).

87. H. Arnold Barton, "Swedish Americans and the Genteel Tradition," *Swedish American Historical Quarterly* (Jan. 2006): 14-32; Barton, "Old Swedish Traditions," 236-240.

88. Johnson, "Origins, Population, Locations," 59-66; Edman, "Organizations," 48-51.

89. Hanson, "The Vasa Order of America," 236-244.

90. Feddersen, *Scandinavians in Michigan*, 266-267. For information on the Vasa Order, see their web page at: www.vasaorder.com.

91. Johnson, "Origins, Population, Locations," 64; "The Smörgåsbord," in *They Made a Difference*, 73-74.

92. "The Smörgåsbord," in *They Made a Difference*, 73-74.

93. Edman, "Organizations," 43-45; Jenny Lind Club of Detroit Collection, Bentley Library, Ann Arbor, Michigan.

94. Johnson, "Origins, Population, Locations," 84-85; Feddersen, *Scandinavians in Michigan*, 246-249; Signe Karlstrom, "The Magic Baton," in *They Made a Difference*, 82-85.

95. A. L. McClain, "Music in Her Soul," in *They Made a Difference*, 107–110.
96. Ibid., 26–37.
97. Signe Karlstrom, "Detroit-Swedish Council," in *They Made a Difference*, 101–105. For information on the Detroit Swedish Council, see also the Detroit Swedish Council Collection, Bentley Library, and http://www.detroitswedishfoundation. com; for the Swedish Council of America, see http://www.swedishcouncil.org.
98. Glenn T. Seaborg, "Swedish Christmas," *Nordstjernan-Svea (North Star)*, 22 Dec. 1966.
99. See for example, "The Swedish Gift to America," (speech to the Vasa Order of America, in Washington, D.C., 1 Oct. 1966), in Glenn T. Seaborg Collection, Northern Michigan University and the Swedish American Council webpage; also Hancks, *Scandinavians in Michigan*, 28–29.
100. Le Roy W. Dahlberg, "Milles at Cranbrook," in *They Made a Difference*, 75–81.
101. For information about the Sweden American Chamber of Commerce-Detroit, see their webpage at www.sacc-usa.org.
102. Detroit Swedish Council, ed., *They Made a Difference*, 96–98; Pamphlet and scrapbook, c. 1977, and "Swedish Heritage Week in Michigan 1984," all in Box 2, Detroit Swedish Council Collection, Bentley Library.
103. Governor Granholm's proclamation can be found at http://www.michigan.gov/ gov/0,1607,7-168-23442_25488_28123-104807-,00.html.
104. For the Swedish American Heritage Society of Western Michigan, see http:// sahswm.org/.
105. Mark Malsee, "Greening the Gov: With Help from Swedes, a Michigan City Goes Biogas!" 6 Nov. 2008, Oh My Gov!, available at http://ohmygov.com/blogs/ general_news/archive/2008/11/06/greening-the-gov-with-help-from-swedes-a-michigan-city-goes-biogas.aspx. For the Bader TV article, 26 Sept. 2008, and a video clip of Gov. Granholm and King Carl XIV Gustaf in Flint, see You Tube, http://www.youtube.com/watch?v=aGpjvvTvM9g.

Appendix 1. The Significance of Ethnic Swedish Food

1. Most websites attribute this poem to either Boone and Erickson (a team of Twin Cities radio announcers who recorded it many years ago) or "Anonymous," but one site states the author was a fellow named Dan Freeburg, "who copyrighted it in 1978 but seems to have given up on enforcing it." (See http://brandywine-books.net/?post_id=428.)

Appendix 2. The Lucia Day Tradition

1. Po Tidholm, "Lucia," and Agneta Lilja, "Lucia December 13th," Sweden, 2004, http://www.sweden.se/eng/Home/Lifestyle/Traditions/Celebrating-the-Swedish-way/Lucia/; "Saint Lucy's Day," *Wikipedia, The Free Encyclopedia*, http://en.wikipedia.org/w/index.php?title=Saint_Lucy%27s_Day&oldid=; Tanya Gulevich, *Encyclopedia of Christmas and New Year's Celebrations* (Detroit: Omnigraphics, 2003), 518–520.

2. H. Arnold Barton, "Old Swedish Traditions," *The Swedish-American Historical Quarterly* 33:4 (Oct. 1982): 236–240.

3. Skulda Banér, *Latchstring Out* (New York: Houghton Mifflin Company, 1944), 124–138.

For Further Reference

Albinson, Grace G. "An Early Swedish Settlement in Michigan." In *American Swedish Historical Foundation Year Book 1947*, part 1. Lancaster, Pennsylvania: Lancaster Press, 1947.

Banér, Skulda. *Latchstring Out.* New York: Houghton Mifflin Company, 1944.

Barton, H. Arnold, ed. *Letters from the Promised Land: Swedes in America, 1840-1914.* Minneapolis: University of Minnesota Press, 1975.

———. "Old Swedish Traditions." *Swedish American Historical Quarterly* 33:4 (Oct. 1982): 236-240.

Beijbom, Ulf. "Swedes." In *Harvard Encyclopedia of American Ethnic Groups*, edited by Stephan Thernstrom, Ann Orlov, and Oscar Handlin. Cambridge: Harvard University Press, 1980.

Benson, Adolph B., and Naboth Hedin. *Swedes in America, 1638-1938.* New York: Haskell House, 1969.

Björk, Ulf Jonas. "The Swedish American Press as an Immigrant Institution." *Swedish American Historical Quarterly* 51:4 (Oct. 2000): 269-282.

Burton, Edward. "The Swedish-American Newspapers in the Sixties and Seventies." *Swedish American Historical Quarterly* (Oct. 2006): 205-217.

Detroit Swedish Council. *They Made a Difference: Highlights of the Swedish Influence on Detroit and Michigan.* Detroit: Detroit Swedish Council, 1976.

Dorson, Richard M. *Bloodstoppers and Bearwalkers: Folk Tales of Canadians, Lum-*

berjacks, and Indians. Cambridge: Harvard University Press, 1972.

Feddersen, Christian T. *Scandinavians in Michigan.* Hancock, Michigan: The Book Concern, 1968.

Forsman, Syrene. "Swedish Finns and Early Ironwood, Michigan." *Swedish Finn Historical Society Quarterly* (Spring 2005): 38, 58.

Fur, Gunlög. "The Making of a Legend: Joe Hill and the I.W.W." *Swedish American Historical Quarterly* 40:3 (July 1989): 101-113.

Hale, Frederick. *Swedes in Wisconsin.* Madison, Wisconsin: Wisconsin Historical Society Press, 2002.

Hancks, Jeffrey W. *Scandinavians in Michigan.* East Lansing: Michigan State University Press, 2006.

Hanson, Henry. "The Vasa Order of America: Its Role in the Swedish-American Community: 1896-1996." *Swedish American Historical Quarterly* 47 (1996): 236-244.

Hoffsten, C. E. "Swedish American History in Lower Michigan." In *The Swedish Element in America: A History of Swedish-American Achievements from 1638 to the Present Day,* 2nd ed., edited by Axel W. Hultén. Chicago: Swedish American Biographical Society, 1934.

Holmio, Armas K. E. *History of the Finns in Michigan,* translated by Ellen M. Ryynanen. Detroit: Wayne State University Press, 2001.

Hokanson, Nels. "Swedes and the I. W. W." *The Swedish Pioneer Historical Quarterly* 23:1 (Jan. 1972): 25-35.

Hultén, Axel W., ed. *The Swedish Element in America: A History of Swedish-American Achievements from 1638 to the Present Day,* 2nd ed. Chicago: Swedish American Biographical Society, 1934.

Janson, Florence E. *The Background of Swedish Immigration.* Chicago: University of Illinois Press, 1931.

Johnson, Clarence H. "Origins, Population, Locations, Occupations and Activities of the Swedes in Detroit." MA thesis, Wayne State University, 1940.

Johnson, Judy M., ed. *Skandia Township Centennial.* Ann Arbor: Braun-Brumfield, 1992.

Kastrup, Allan. *The Swedish Heritage in America.* St. Paul: North Central, 1975.

Lankton, Larry. *Cradle to Grave: Life, Work, and Death in the Lake Superior Copper Mines.* Cambridge: Oxford University Press, 1991.

Myhrman, Anders. "The Finland-Swedes in America." *Swedish American Historical Quarterly* 31:1 (Jan. 1980): 16-33.

———. *Finlandssvenskar I Amerika: The Finland Swedes in America.* Helsingfors, Finland: Svenska Litteratursallskapet i Finland, 1973.

———. "Swedish Finns and Iron Mountain." Translated by Syrene Forsman. *Swedish Finn Historical Society Quarterly* (Summer 2005): 68-69.

Nelson, Edward O. "Recollections of the Salvation Army's Scandinavian Corps." *Swedish American Historical Quarterly* 29:4 (Oct. 1978): 257-276.

Olsson, Nils William. "The Swedish Settlement of Tustin, MI." *The Swedish Pioneer* 12:3 (July 1962): 109-117.

Peano, Shirley. "Swedish Settlement in Marquette County." *Harlow's Wooden Man* 8:4 (Fall 1972): 6-7.

Redmond, Jeffrey R. *"Viking" Hoaxes in North America.* New York: Carlton, 1979.

Stephenson, George M. *The Religious Aspects of Swedish Immigration: A Study of Immigrant Churches.* Minneapolis: University of Minnesota Press, 1932.

Williams, Anna. "Journalism and Ethnicity in Swedish America." *Swedish American Historical Quarterly* 43 (1992): 146-155.

Winquist, Alan H. *Swedish American Landmarks.* Minneapolis: Swedish Council of America, 1995.

Index